INNOVATING TO ZERO

Praise for *Innovating to Zero*

'*Innovating to Zero* is, arguably, the next big idea originating from India since jugaad innovation. It is bold and sweeping in its vision, tackling large-scale challenges like zero emissions, zero waste and zero poverty. By embracing structured, systemic innovation, this philosophy fosters transformative, sustainable progress that truly addresses problems at their core.'

—**Vikas Sehgal**, global partner and vice chairman, Rothschild & Co; independent director of the board for Novelis and Cyient

'Sarwant has, for as long as I've known him, had the ability to grasp the big picture and commit to an audacious plan. *Innovating to Zero* is an example of that; shaping a future full of zeros: zero emissions, zero congestion, zero accidents, you name it. In a beautifully crafted book, Sarwant goes on to give examples of how this drive to zero can be achieved. He cites our interaction with the Nissan LEAF, arguably the first zero-emission mass production car. And at Switch, together we created the world's first zero-emissions commercial vehicle company. Sarwant's book captures these stories and more and inspires us all to strive for zero.'

—**Andy Palmer**, former CEO, Aston Martin; former COO, Nissan Motor Company; former CEO, Switch Mobility; chairman, Inobat Auto; chairman, PodPoint PLC; chairman, HiLo; chairman Ionetic Ltd; chairman, Brill Power Ltd

'In his engaging and timely book, Sarwant Singh explores the transformative concept of *Innovating to Zero*, illustrating how it can be applied across diverse domains. Leveraging his long-time expertise in the automotive industry, Singh examines how the sector is addressing critical challenges with its drive towards zero traffic accidents, zero emissions and zero congestion. The book's true value lies in its actionable, step-by-step framework, providing a practical roadmap for effectively implementing this visionary approach.'

—**Michael Hawes OBE**, chief executive, The Society of Motor Manufacturers and Traders Limited, UK

'Given the turbulent times we live in, never has the message being espoused by *Innovating to Zero* been more needed. Sarwant challenges us all to look radically at every aspect of our business and life to strive to be the best version of ourselves.'

—**Parminder Kohli**, UK country chair , EVP Sustainability and Carbon, Shell

'As humanity faces increasingly complex challenges, innovative solutions are critical. Sarwant Singh's book highlights the role of human ingenuity and foresight in transforming this vision into actionable strategies. Presented in a clear and accessible style, this work makes sophisticated concepts comprehensible to a broad audience, bridging the gap between visionary ideas and practical implementation.'

—**Sanjay Brahmawar**, former CEO of Software AG, NED at HERE Technologies; board of trustees, Frankfurt School of Finance

INNOVATING TO ZERO

A ZERO VISION STRATEGY FOR CONSCIOUSLY CREATING A BETTER WORLD

SARWANT SINGH

HarperCollins *Publishers* India

First published in India by HarperCollins *Publishers* 2025
HarperCollins *Publishers* India, Cyber City,
Building 10-A, Gurugram, Haryana – 122002, India

www.harpercollins.co.in

2 4 6 8 10 9 7 5 3 1

P-ISBN: 978-93-6989-463-5
E-ISBN: 978-93-6989-220-4

Typeset in 11.5/15.2 Minion Pro
by HarperCollins *Publishers* India Pvt. Ltd

Printed and bound at
Replika Press Pvt. Ltd.

FSC www.fsc.org MIX Paper | Supporting responsible forestry FSC™ C016779

This book is produced from independently certified FSC® paper to ensure responsible forest management.

HarperCollins *Publishers*, Macken House, 39/40 Mayor Street Upper,
Dublin 1, D01 C9W8, Ireland

To the two most important women in my life—my mother,
Gurcharan Kaur, and my wife, Julia Saini.
I miss you, mum.

The detailed notes pertaining to this book are available on the HarperCollins website. Scan this QR code to access the same.

CONTENTS

FOREWORD

We are living in an era of unprecedented change, where the only constant is uncertainty. The foundations of our societies, economies and industries are shifting at an extraordinary pace. Businesses, governments and individuals adapt or risk becoming obsolete. Traditional models are being swept away by disruptive forces such as artificial intelligence, geopolitical instability, climate crises and evolving consumer expectations.

This volatile landscape requires a new approach that does not merely react to change but actively shapes it. *Innovating to Zero* represents such a mindset. It is a forward-looking strategy that converts challenges into opportunities, ensuring both sustainability and long-term competitive advantage. In a world that has evolved from traditional models, the ability to achieve zero—whether in emissions, waste or inefficiencies—is profound it is potential for transformation.

This is why *Innovating to Zero: A Zero-Vision Strategy for Consciously Creating a Better World* is such a critical and timely book. Sarwant Singh, a respected automotive industry insider and futurist, has long been at the forefront of identifying transformative trends. His journey began more than a decade ago with *New Mega Trends* in 2012 and, with his latest offering, he takes an even bolder step by exploring how zero is more than just a sustainability check box. It reflects a paradigm shift in how we live, work, think and create. Going beyond carbon-neutral factories and green technologies, he envisions zero as a force that can redefine industries, disrupt conventional thinking and shape a better future for humanity.

As this book makes clear, zero vision is not just about business, it is about society. In terms of the former, it challenges industries to move beyond incremental progress and embrace disruptive innovations that deliver lasting impact. It reveals how zero can drive meaningful change across healthcare, energy, education, industry and technology sectors. Equally, it delves into how the philosophy can alchemize positive societal outcomes, improving equity, quality of life and long-term well-being. Importantly, this book is not a compendium of abstract theories but a practical guide that offers a structured framework, case studies and actionable insights on how to build a zero-vision strategy in the real world.

Nowhere is this more relevant than in the automotive industry, which faces the critical challenges of emissions, congestion and highway safety. As a pioneer in the zero-vision movement, the industry is already pushing boundaries with carbon-neutral factories and zero-emission vehicles. But true transformation requires going further. What if cars were designed not just for sustainability but also for accessibility and inclusivity to accommodate different social groups? What if vehicles were equipped with customized health and wellness features that could enhance the safety, comfort and overall well-being of vehicle occupants? Hyundai Motor Company has a very compelling vision of the future where mobility is safer, more sustainable and more convenient. Similarly, *Innovating to Zero* expands the role of mobility beyond the sphere of transportation, envisioning it as a catalyst for social change. Indeed, to remain competitive, organizations should consider integrating 'Innovating to Zero' into their DNA, not as a siloed initiative, but as a core principle guiding sustainability commitments.

At Hyundai, this all-embracing philosophy extends beyond sustainability, similar to the broader principles of zero that Sarwant explores in this book. We have committed to achieving carbon neutrality by 2045, eliminating CO_2 emissions at every stage of production and operation. Under our vision 'Progress for Humanity', we are shaping a zero-emission future by investing heavily in battery-electric and hydrogen fuel-cell technology. By 2035, all new Hyundai vehicles sold in Europe will be electric. We are also working to offer a full lineup of 21 EV models, targeting annual sales of two million electric vehicles as early as 2030.

Beyond passenger mobility, we are leading zero-emission innovation in commercial transportation. In 2024, we launched the NorCAL ZERO Project, deploying thirty Class 8 XCIENT Fuel Cell trucks—the largest commercial deployment of hydrogen-powered fuel cell electric trucks in the US. This initiative is reshaping freight transportation in California, reducing emissions in a crucial logistics corridor.

Our ZER01NE programme fosters creative ecosystems, funding start-ups and innovators at the intersection of art, technology and mobility. Each year, ZERO1NE Day celebrates the breakthroughs emerging from this collaborative effort. Meanwhile, Hyundai Mobis is redefining vehicle innovation with technologies like the Zero Turn system, which allows all four wheels to rotate 90 degrees for effortless movement in tight spaces. By integrating electrification and autonomous driving, this technology represents the next frontier of purpose-built mobility. For us, at Hyundai, Zero is the foundation of a smarter, cleaner and more connected future.

And, finally, the many success stories highlighted in this book demonstrate that change is driven by visionary leadership. This book challenges leaders to ask: Does our organization have their CXOs focused on zero strategy or its equivalent? Are we setting measurable zero targets for employees? Are we empowering our teams to drive long-term impact for both business and society? These will be the defining questions of leadership in the new era.

For those who care about the future of our industry, our company, and the world, *Innovating to Zero* can help all of us find best practices as we navigate a world of profound transformation. And, crucially, it can help us reshape our future in ways we are only beginning to imagine.

José Muñoz, chief executive officer,
Hyundai Motor Company

PREFACE

A Day in the Life of Leyla in a Zero-Vision World

It's just your typical day in 2040 … a day full of zeros.

Welcome to the year 2040. Zeros have taken over—in a good way. Imagine a world where every aspect of life revolves around the concept of zero. And no, I'm not talking about a day where nothing happens or where I've forgotten all my passwords! I'm talking about my day: a day in the life of a young woman living in a world where zero is the ultimate goal.

My day starts, like many of yours, with a voice—not an alarm, but a greeting from Adele. Yes, *the* Adele, who's still waking me up with her soulful melodies, though now with a little help from my AI companion, Amelie, who knows my musical tastes inside out. Amelie isn't just any digital assistant; she's my personal guide through this zero-vision world. And on this special day—my thirty-first birthday—Amelie has already lined up a day that's bursting with zeros.

'Good morning, Leyla! It's 16 January 2040, and guess what? You're officially thirty-one today! But don't worry, your biological age is still a sprightly twenty-five. Your health is looking great, except for that tiny hundred gram gain since yesterday. Not to worry, I've got a diet plan that'll knock that double zero back into place. Oh, and by the way, your zero-emission electric car is fully charged, and there's zero traffic today, so enjoy your drive!'

As I savour my zero-sugar beet smoothie and grab my net zero-carbon bircher muesli, I check the smart energy monitor. Zero energy wastage, and an extra 10 kWh of energy generated by my solar panels over the last twenty-four hours. It's no surprise; I've always been an advocate for sustainability like many of my Gen-Z-er friends, inspired as we have been by climate change activist, Greta Thunberg.

A quick video call to my parents—I like the new, upgraded Li-Fi broadband in my home which supports zero latency when it comes to using devices—reveals a birthday surprise: a trip to Copenhagen, the world's first carbon-neutral capital. I'm thrilled since I've never been, and the thought of sipping a net zero beer in a carbon-neutral brewery is enough to make anyone excited. Around 75 per cent of the city's residents cycle, all vehicles are electric, and the city recycles everything. In contrast, my home city of London is still a decade behind its commitment to becoming fully carbon-neutral. Before leaving, I make sure my garbage is sorted for the neighborhood's zero-waste initiative: everything is reused, repaired or recycled. No waste here.

As I head out, Amelie, ever the diligent assistant, reminds me of my 8 a.m. work call to discuss the progress on our zero-cancer project. She also gives me a heads-up that my friends are planning a surprise tonight ... perhaps starting with a performance at the Royal Opera House, which recently achieved net zero emissions, followed by dinner at a trendy tapas bar known for its zero carbon footprint.

I quickly dial into the work call, while still finishing up at home. And then, as I slide into the car, the call effortlessly transfers to the car's digital suite. With my focus now fully on the call, I'm grateful for the little things—how the car's temperature is set just right, not too hot or too cold, because who has time to fiddle with dials these days? The car even takes care of setting the house alarm that I, of course, forgot to activate in my morning rush. And as if on cue, Amelie orders my zero dairy, zero sugar caffe Americano to be ready for pick-up in twenty minutes.

My drive to the office is smooth and efficient, thanks to zero traffic congestion and my Level 4 autonomous vehicle. The M25, that my Dad once referred to as the UK's largest car park, now boasts zero accidents with zero fatalities in three years—a testament to the power of autonomous technology. The UK's national highway authorities have successfully replicated Vision Zero, Sweden's pioneering road traffic safety project of the 1990s. I often wonder though why the 70 mph speed limit instituted on UK's motorways since 1965 has not been raised, particularly with the kind of progress that we've seen with automotive safety technologies. I fleetingly watch a few electric vertical take-off and landing vehicles (eVTOLS) soar above and marvel, both literally and metaphorically, at how high we have aimed and far we've come.

While my car takes care of the drive to the office, my thoughts drift to a little lunchtime retail therapy. My mantra? Be a zero consumer—minimizing my environmental impact and championing sustainability with every purchase. It's my way of reducing waste and shrinking my environmental footprint to, you guessed it, zero. I only shop at places that share my values and are as committed to sustainability as I am.

Take my favourite clothing store that is dedicated to the three Rs of repair, reduce and recycle, and champions circular fashion.

Every time I pick up a pre-owned piece, it comes in eco-friendly packaging that is either recyclable, compostable, biodegradable or reusable. It's guilt-free shopping at its best.

Another store that I enjoy frequenting has mastered the art of blending cutting-edge technology with good old-fashioned customer service, creating a personalized shopping experience that feels both futuristic and friendly. Robots whiz around, managing inventory, fixing out-of-place items and analysing customer preferences.

I'm always amazed at how this store gets the latest runway trends onto its racks faster than you can say 'wardrobe malfunction'. With zero design-to-shelf response time, that smart trench coat I spotted on a model last week? It's probably already waiting for me. Beyond the clothes, they've smartly reserved the tech for where it matters most, like self-service payment kiosks and return stations. For the stuff that counts, like finding that perfect shade of lipstick or navigating the digital experience, they've still got sales associates to give expert advice. Last week, they even helped me pick out a stunning red dress. It needed a few tweaks, but no worries—zero turnaround times. Now that's what I call next-level zero stress retail therapy.

For tonight's dinner, I think I will wear my favourite regenerated cashmere top with my vegetarian leather skirt. It'll be an appropriate match for the tapas bar which is zero central—and, by that, I don't mean calories. The food is always fresh, sourced locally, organically grown and seasonal. And the restaurant itself? Powered entirely by renewable, solar energy, with zero waste (seriously, no bins in sight), and furniture that is all upcycled or recycled. Plus, they follow zero prejudice hiring practices. Every detail is designed to make you feel good about your choices—from the food on your plate to the people serving it.

While I anticipate a fun evening, I still need to get through a regular workday first. My office is in a zero-carbon building that generates net-positive energy. We are a zero-paper and (nearly) zero-emails office. We have zero turnaround time on projects since technology helps with business decisions and processes in real time. I am happy to note that this typically means zero client complaints.

My company is at the forefront of the healthcare industry, developing next-generation drugs, medtech devices, and health, wellness, and wellbeing solutions. We are striving towards zero obesity, zero infections and even zero diseases. Humans have already eradicated smallpox and malaria, and now, we're on the brink of even bigger breakthroughs. A world with zero pandemics, superbugs and mutating viruses? Now that's something to look forward to.

To ensure that our innovations reach their full potential, our production processes embrace the philosophy of zero defects—a 'first-time-right' quality strategy, among the oldest zero-based concepts in manufacturing. Zero defect manufacturing, or ZDM as it is commonly known, is a cornerstone of our operations, reflecting our pursuit of perfection.

This same commitment extends to our research and development. By integrating state-of-the-art technology and data-driven approaches, we're innovating to zero in medical research, aiming for nothing less than transformative outcomes for patients worldwide. We are constantly pushing the boundaries on what's possible with our pioneering work on human augmentation, brain-machine interfaces, advanced prosthetics, cognitive enhancement and enhanced sensory systems. My dad often remarks that we're taking humanity from transhumanism to the evolutionary future of extropianism.

As my day unfolds, it's clear that this will be—as it usually is—a day full of zeros. But these zeros aren't empty; they're filled with possibility, hope and innovation. So, as you turn the pages of this book, imagine a world where zero isn't just a number, but a reality. As, in 2040, zero is everywhere.

Note: The concepts in this book have been elucidated through tables and figures. However, given the print-layout limitations and for clarity, please refer to them on the sources mentioned.

1

INTRODUCTION

Zero: The Idea of Nothing and Everything

Zero. What would we do without it? Unique, ubiquitous and utterly indispensable.

From its early use as a placeholder in Mesopotamian and Mayan civilizations to being ascribed value in seventh-century India, from being embraced by China and the Middle East in the eighth century to finally reaching Western Europe in the twelfth century, zero has become the foundation without which the modern world could crumble.[1]

From being represented as an angled double wedge or dots to its current avatar as an oval, its form has evolved. From being used in mathematics to finding its way into science, philosophy, economics, engineering, software and quantum computing, the zero has, well, come full circle. Not bad for a digit that, historically, was the last to come into use.

Nil. Oh. O. Cipher. Naught. Nought. Void. Zip. Nada. Zilch. A stack of synonyms for a number that means 'nothing' and indicates an absence of value. But, as we all know, zero is among the most powerful and versatile concepts that exists today, the bedrock of multiple disciplines in our modern world.

The Significance of Zero

The most obvious presence of zero is in mathematics, where it is used as an integer, a placeholder in place value systems (as James Bond might attest, 007 is very different from 700), and to carry out fundamental arithmetic operations.

It is a foundational concept in algebra, geometry and calculus. These three disciplines, in turn, are the pillars of physics, chemistry, biology, automation, engineering, economics, finance, accounting and much, much more.

In the sciences, zero is used as a reference point to measure various parameters. It is the freezing point of water on the Celsius scale, while absolute zero on the kelvin scale marks the lowest temperature possible. It is also used to test principles, such as zero-point energy theories in quantum mechanics.

In digital computing, zero, along with one, is the foundation of binary code. This means that if you are reading this book on a digital device, you have zero to thank.

We would all be hopelessly lost without zero. GPS systems and maps, after all, rely on the idea that the equator is at zero degrees latitude and the prime meridian at zero degrees longitude.

The zero-energy universe theory suggests that the total amount of energy in the universe—positive and negative—balances off to reach exactly zero. Much like a zero-sum game, where gains and losses are exactly even, so the net change is zero.

Zero-rated goods and services are exempt from value-added taxation (VAT) because they are considered essential and vital cogs in manufacturing ecosystems.

Ground zero is defined as the starting point or base for an activity. It is, as Oppenheimer might have noted, also the point on the earth's surface directly above or below an exploding nuclear bomb.

In history, Year Zero marked the rather dire start to the rule of the genocidal Khmer Rouge regime in Cambodia where families, hospitals, intelligentsia, education, factories, music, religion, money, marriage, civil and political rights were denounced.

On a more optimistic note, parliamentarians in India wait for zero hour when issues of urgent importance are raised and discussed.

From countries to clothes, there is no escaping that little oval. Size zero is the smallest size of women's clothes, meant for extremely thin women.

Then there are the more esoteric notions of zero. Numerology holds that zero signals a future of (mostly good) possibilities. In particular, a repeating sequence like '000' is considered an 'angel' number.[2] I would be overjoyed to see such 'angel' numbers added to my publishing advance and to the sales of this book.

In Indian culture and philosophy, the concept of 'shunya' (the Sanskrit word for zero) means the idea of emptiness or a void denoting an absence of ego, a sense of detachment. In essence, the idea of everything in nothingness.

But that's not all.

Vision Zero in the Twenty-First Century

In keeping with the changing needs of the twenty-first century—twenty centuries each of hundred years (plenty of zeros here as well)—zero is transforming. It is still very much at the core of everything, except now as the lynchpin of an entirely new set of ideas.

If the last decade was all about digital computing and the binary digit, that is, the bit, then the coming one will be about quantum computing and the quantum bit, that is, the qubit. Unlike the bit, which can be *either* zero or one, the qubit can be *both* zero and one, simultaneously, until measured. Much like the wealth of opportunities this opens, zero too is unveiling astonishing possibilities—a vision zero, if you will.

What is this vision zero? What began as a goal of making roads safer—zero fatalities, zero road accidents, zero serious traffic injuries—has now grown in scope and scale. Today, the vision-zero world is all-encompassing, embracing manufacturing, retail, cities, individuals, corporates, governments, work, home, leisure, products, performance, processes and more. It is about a philosophy that pivots around safe, smart and sustainable practices. Beyond the objective of achieving carbon neutrality and net zero, it is about consciously building a better world. A world free of errors, defects and negatives.

So think: zero emissions, zero accidents, zero waste, zero crimes, zero hunger, zero poverty, zero illiteracy, zero diseases, zero carbon, factories, countries and, possibly, Earth.

Realizing this ambitious vision requires innovative mindsets, technologies, business models, strategies and solutions. Which invariably brings us to the question: How does one 'innovate to zero'?

2

DESTINATION ZERO: THE VISION

It was more than a decade ago that I first heard the term 'innovating to zero'. In 2010, against the shadow of looming climate change, Bill Gates spoke of the need for an 'energy miracle'. His TED Talk—'Innovating to Zero'—touched on the importance of working towards zero-carbon energy and slashing 80 per cent of carbon emissions by 2050.[1] He advocated an advanced nuclear energy technology called the Travelling Wave Reactor that would be safe, scalable, reliable and have zero emissions.

I will admit it wasn't so much the technology as the vision behind it that gave me pause for thought. Innovating to zero was unquestionably a great idea. But how did one get there? Indeed, what piqued my interest was Gates' admission that delivering on humanity's zero carbon energy dreams would require Tony Stark levels of 'massive innovation'. What would this entail? Where could such innovation be applied? Could this audacious vision succeed? If so, why, how and where?

Let me be clear, my quest for answers continues. Much of this has to do with the fact that its applicability has evolved in ways unimaginable a decade ago. For a start, it is no longer only about clean energy. Instead, it is, as I briefly touched upon in the previous chapter, about envisioning a more comprehensive, picture-perfect world via an innovating-to-zero lens.

In my first book, *New Mega Trends: Implications for our Future Lives*, published in 2012, I described innovating to zero as I would even today, a good decade later: as an all-embracing mega vision.[2] A dream of an ideal world, a desire for perfection in our society and businesses, and in every product and service that we consume. A zero-concept world without crimes, diseases, hunger, social and economic inequities, emissions, and that final boundary, death. If that sounds like utopia, well, that's the general idea.

Which leads us to the obvious question: can this model be put into practice? My unequivocal answer is yes. You need only look at the growing number of individuals, investors, institutions, companies, cities and countries who have avidly embraced the promise of innovating to zero.

The concept is endless in its possibilities. And if you don't believe me, just do what I did—carry out an internet search to identify its potential applications in the industrial and services world. What came up was an astonishing list of over a hundred possibilities, and counting. From innovating to zero applied to accidents, waste, emissions, defects, downtime, inventory, time to market, overproduction, cost overruns, impact operations, technology gaps and talent churn, it would appear that there was not a single area where the idea was not relevant.

While I will go into greater detail about innovating to zero in specific industries in the subsequent chapters, here, I will just touch briefly upon its use in key sectors.

Retail

In the retail sector, innovating to zero would, ideally, embrace zero-carbon concepts from energy use to supply chains, products to packaging. But achieving zero in its entirety is not without its challenges and so, what we have been seeing is incremental, rather than any big-bang change across various aspects of retail.

If I were to pick a winner of the vision zero in this section, it would be outdoor-apparel maker, Patagonia, which, long before it became buzzworthy among corporates, stood for sustainability and responsible consumption. Patagonia is a certified B Corp whose business model successfully aligns profitability with social and environmental performance, transparency and accountability. Led by iconic founder–owner Yvon Chouinard, Patagonia was an early standard bearer for a range of social and environmental initiatives, precursors of various ideas that feed, one way or another, into the current understanding of innovating to zero. These initiatives range from the Worn Wear programme that encourages customers to buy used products to the '1% for the Planet' project where 1 per cent of sales are channeled to 'grassroots environmental groups making a difference in their local communities'. Patagonia also supports regenerative organic-farming practices, focuses on repair, reduce, and recycle practices, and promotes circular models. Tellingly, Chouinard transferred ownership of his over five decade old $3 billion company to a trust that will oversee an estimated $100 million being disbursed to climate change prevention measures and to protect undeveloped land.[3] A great example of innovating to zero philanthropy.

Zero-carbon shops—retail establishments with net zero-carbon emissions and zero-carbon products—are still a work in progress. In April 2023, India got its first Apple store in Mumbai. Besides snazzy architecture and cool Apple merchandise, what stood out was that it was India's first carbon-neutral store that runs on 100 per cent renewable energy. In September 2023, Apple made another splash with its carbon-neutral Apple Watches, whose design innovations and clean energy sources slashed product emissions by three-quarters in each of these watches.[4]

These steps are adding up to Apple's eventual goal of becoming carbon neutral across its entire business—the products themselves and their entire life cycle as well as the overall manufacturing supply chain—by 2030.

However, one could say Apple is a little late to the party. Way back in 2011, UK multinational retailer Marks and Spencer (M&S) launched what it advertised as 'high street's first-ever carbon neutral bra.'[5] Manufactured in a carbon-neutral factory in Sri Lanka and using a judicious mix of renewable energy sources, sustainable manufacturing and carbon offsets, M&S achieved a zero-carbon footprint for its bra. What made this an impressive feat was the supply chain complexity involved: the bra itself had twenty-one components sourced from twelve different suppliers and included lace—one of the most carbon-intensive materials to produce. Simultaneously, tree planting, sustainable agriculture, wildlife protection, and community building initiatives that went with the whole project got a much-needed boost. On a larger scale, M&S has committed to becoming net zero in carbon emissions across its operations, supply chain and products by 2040.

From high-street to high-end retail. British luxury brand Burberry asserted that during April 2021–March 2022, it achieved its goal of becoming carbon neutral across its global operations and, moreover, switched over to 100 per cent renewable electricity.[6] It also laid claim to becoming the first luxury fashion brand to receive Science Based Targets initiative (SBTi) approval for its net zero emissions goals.

Other companies like everyone's favorite DIY go-to, IKEA; consumer goods giant, Unilever; and sporting shoes and apparel behemoth, Nike have set ambitious sustainability agendas centred on eventually getting to zero. IKEA, for instance, has committed to not just being carbon neutral but becoming carbon positive by 2030.[7] Renewable energy, recycled materials, sustainable design and energy-efficient stores are all part of the plan. Unilever's 'planet plans' focus on achieving zero emissions in operations by 2030 and net zero emissions by 2039.[8] Nike's Move to Zero underlines its quest for zero carbon and zero waste, while 'helping to protect the future of sport'.[9]

Since we are talking of innovating to zero, I must reference its originator, Bill Gates' Microsoft. The tech major has stated its objective of becoming a carbon negative, water positive and zero-waste company by 2030.[10] It has committed to removing all the carbon it has emitted either directly or indirectly through electrical consumption over the past fifty odd years (yes, Microsoft is that old!) by 2050. In pursuit of this objective, Xbox has become the first major gaming console to create energy and emissions measurement tools. A slew of interventions like greening game code and energy-saver modes have, moreover, enabled savings of over 1.2 million metric tons of CO_2e, compared to usage without interventions.[11]

PepsiCo has set a goal to design 100 per cent of its packaging to be recyclable, compostable, biodegradable or reusable by 2025. Its positive (pep+) agenda has set an objective to become net zero by 2040, initially by ensuring significant emission reductions within the value chain, further reinforced by limited use of carbon-removal offsets to balance residual emissions.

That's not all. Spanish fast-fashion brand Zara, whose breakneck speed of commercialization of designs is based on a combination of customer feedback and data analysis, exemplifies the drive to get to zero design-to-shelves response times. The company's extremely agile and responsive business model means that clothes are in stores within ten days to a fortnight, in comparison to the protracted, often months-long lead time required by other fashion stores to design and retail new lines. Zara introduces around a thousand new styles every month, compared to competing brands that manage an average of about three thousand annually.[12] What emerges is a strong business case for retailers to adopt zero design-to-shelves time as it provides instant RoI; you sell what is in fashion, you sell what your customers desire and you do so with the need for zero inventory management. Zara has got its game right: it posted a neat $2.7 billion in net profits in H1 2023.[13]

Table 2.1 shows the zeros that can be applied to the retail industry.

Table 2.1: Zero in Retail		
Zero inventory	Zero-contact returns	Zero-discrimination retail
Zero-waste retail	Zero-cash transactions	Zero-package shopping
Zero-contact shopping	Zero tolerance for counterfeit products	Zero customer complaints
Zero-checkout lines	Zero-surcharge pricing	Zero-checkout experience
Zero-markup pricing	Zero-touch check-in	Zero-plastic display materials
Zero-interest financing	Zero-loss supply chain	Zero-disruption retail events
Zero-returns policies	Zero-plastic packaging	Zero-waste shopping carts
Zero-touch shopping	Zero-wait shopping	Zero-wait returns
Zero-friction customer experience	Zero-cost returns	Zero-contact personal shopping
Zero-packaging retail	Zero-preservatives food retail	Zero-advertising footprint
Zero-contact delivery	Zero-preservatives food retail	Zero-sales pressure environment

Zero-queue shopping	Zero-hassle membership programmes	Zero-error inventory management
Zero-shelf stocking	Zero-marketing waste	Zero-waste shopping bags
Zero-paper receipts	Zero-downtime retail technology	Zero-carbon emission delivery

Add to the list, zero shrinkage, which would imply the absence of inventory losses caused by shoplifting, employee theft, administrative error or vendor fraud. While these are all to the good, one innovating-to-zero concept that I am sure is likely to face a chilly reception is: zero discounts! That said, just imagine what it could do to your brand and bottom line if every store worldwide practiced a same-price policy with zero discounts all year around.

Manufacturing

Carbon-neutral factories or net zero factories made their debut when Volvo Trucks announced the setting up of the world's first carbon-neutral factory in Ghent, Belgium, way back in 2007. Renewables were the sole source of energy. Since those early days, this vision zero in manufacturing has gone purposefully mainstream and is the vision set by European Union to guide what is now termed Industry 5.0.

The food and beverage industry is a prominent vision zero adherent in its manufacturing practices, constantly looking at ways to reduce food waste, improve packaging, employ sustainable agricultural sourcing practices and streamline supply change management. Juice company, Innocent Drinks, which will be celebrating its quarter century this year, is a certified B Corp. It has a target of net zero by 2040, champions sustainable farming and is pushing to create a truly circular economy for its packaging. It plans to make bottles out of 100 per cent renewable or recycled material, avoiding the use of virgin oil-based plastics by 2030. It has set up one of the world's first carbon-neutral juice factories, the 'blender'.[14] Located in the port city of Rotterdam, the focus is on maximizing resource efficiency, using heavy-duty, zero-emission electric trucks for transport, and minimizing energy consumption and waste. Similarly, albeit on a much larger scale, Swiss food and beverage giant, Nestlé, is working on its zero profile. It has indicated a shift away from the use of carbon offsets to achieve carbon-neutral brands, focusing instead on actual emissions reductions in its operations and value chain. The company's roadmap includes achieving net zero greenhouse gas (GHG) emissions by 2050 and realizing 50 per cent emissions reductions by 2030.[15]

German technology leader Siemens has committed to ensuring that its worldwide production facilities and buildings achieve net zero carbon footprint by 2030. It is investing €650 million and leveraging its own technologies in the push towards decarbonization.[16] Underlining its credentials as a sustainability focused company, Siemens is a signatory to SBTi and the Paris Climate Agreement on climate-control measures, in addition to global initiatives like RE100, EV100 and EP100.

Apart from carbon-neutral factories, the manufacturing sector has embraced the grail of Zero Defects Manufacturing (ZDM) or the 'first-time-right' quality strategy, among the most well-established zero-driven concepts in the manufacturing sector.

The concept made its first appearance over four decades ago in Philip Crosby's 14-step quality improvement programme with steps 7 (Plan for Zero Defects Program) and 9 (Zero Defects Day) relating to zero defects. Since then, this innovating-to-zero philosophy has evolved from a theoretical concept to a quality-improvement mechanism and, from thereon, to its current incarnation as a full-fledged business and manufacturing strategy.

The essence of the zero defects or zero faults or zero errors concept is simple: you innovate towards manufacturing a perfect product without defects, a strategy that would need the highest quality-control standards. It is an idea that is critical to literally every sphere, from pharmaceuticals and medical devices to spacecraft and missiles. I sometimes wish I had such an inbuilt process to save me from my frequent culinary disasters, where the process of converting a mouthwatering recipe into a delectable dish somehow goes awry.

The first implementation of the zero defects concept recorded in corporate history is, perhaps, the quality-control programme deployed by the Denver branch of Lockheed Martin (then Martin Marietta Corporation) in the late 1960s on the Titan Missile project.[17] However, it was launched more as a motivational exercise than a quality-control programme, as the 100 per cent defect-free vision was then perceived as an impossibility by quality-control professionals. The programme fizzled out because it was understood to be just that—a mere 'programme' and not a way of running one's business that one would innovate to.

Variants of this zero-defects concept have since found their way into different business and production strategies. Toyota had its zero-defects campaign in the 1960s, while Motorola created a disruptive buzz with its Six Sigma strategy in the late 1980s. According to this manufacturing strategy, which is typically a statistical model, Six Sigma would result in the production of 99.99966 per cent of defect-free goods, translating to an impressive 3.4 defects for every million products produced. Today, Six Sigma certifications continue to be wielded with as much pride as the receipt of a black belt in martial arts. More recently, of course, the spotlight has been on Lean Production and Total

Quality Management (TQM) as a way of working towards a zero-defect vision.

ZDM is now looking at the complete elimination of defects through a multi-pronged approach where zero is achieved not only through identification and rectification of defective products and processes but, more proactively, through prediction and prevention as well. Is this vision of zero defects truly achievable? I would hesitate to say a definitive 'yes', but what is clear is that a clutch of enabling technologies, such as data analytics and digital manufacturing, are moving the needle ever closer to the grail of 100 per cent defect-free manufacturing.

Energy

As mentioned earlier, innovating to zero was first attributed to an advanced nuclear energy–based, zero-emission technology, the Travelling Wave Reactor, developed by TerraPower. Backed by Bill Gates, the company's goal has been to provide 'safe, affordable and abundant carbon-free energy'. Advanced nuclear technology besides, other popular forms of zero-emission technologies include wind, solar, geothermal, wave, tidal and ocean thermal energy, to name a few.

In terms of the transmission and distribution (T&D) side of the energy industry, zero transmission and distribution losses, coupled with zero load-shedding and zero energy thefts, are ideas that are increasingly being implemented on an ad-hoc basis in cities that are aiming for no losses during the process of energy distribution.

Several countries have a policy vision for an energy-progressive society, free from fossil fuels and dependence on imported energy. The UK, for instance, has stated it remains committed to becoming net zero by 2050,[18] although it has pared back on some plans stating the need for a 'fairer' and more 'realistic' approach to ease the burden on working people. Plans to boost energy security and push to net zero include: a spatial plan for energy infrastructure to provide clarity to energy industry participants and consumers; a 'fast track' process for nationally important transmission infrastructure projects to ensure they are prioritized and to help businesses and households connect to the grid sooner; and a new approach to grid connections, where energy projects that are ready first will connect first and get online faster.

Across the world, energy diversification and energy efficiency are the fulcrum of ambitious targets to achieve carbon neutrality or significantly reduce carbon emissions. Norway is aiming for carbon neutrality by 2030, Finland by 2035 and Iceland by 2040, while New Zealand and Canada are aiming to achieve net-zero carbon emissions by 2050. This transition will be catalysed by the use of clean energy, along with smart transmission and distribution.

In Chapter 5 of this book, we will delve into what the future of energy will look, how innovating to zero will shape the energy industry in the twenty-first century, and how energy could be potentially made available for free in the years to come. Imagine what that would mean: paying zero tariff for energy. Some industries like hydrogen will take off and we could hit our targets of climate change without much ado.

Healthcare

There are two major aspects of innovating to zero to consider in the healthcare arena. The first, more immediate and achievable, is that of the hospital itself. Much like in other construction builds, net-zero hospitals will use zero-carbon materials, energy-efficient building designs and smart building systems. Reinforcing this will be renewable energy sources and smart heating, ventilation and air conditioning (HVAC) systems.

The other, more long-term, aspect relates to actual healthcare-related procedures like zero-invasive surgery or, even more ambitiously, zero surgical errors. There's also the challenge to get to zero medical waste. I would love if there were some way hospitals (especially in the UK) could figure out zero waiting times and zero billing queues.

On a far more sweeping scale, there could be the vision of zero diseases. The once-in-a-lifetime pandemic notwithstanding, I think we have made tremendous progress in tackling more traditional diseases like malaria and polio. To date, only two diseases can lay claim to have achieved the zero milestone of complete eradication—smallpox and rinderpest.

Countries like Saudi Arabia and the UK are giving us a glimpse into a future of zero obesity. Grappling with an obesity epidemic and the healthcare burden it entails, Saudi Arabia has increased 'sin' taxes on fatty foods. The Health Survey for England for 2021 reported that 64 per cent of adults were overweight or obese,[19] prompting calls for government intervention in the form of punitive taxes on foods with higher levels of salt, sugar and fat.

In positive signs, certain zero-calorie foods are already very popular, and we have also seen success with branded drinks like Coke Zero and Pepsi Black. I expect more branding of foods and beverages around the zero concept in future.

Buildings

The building sector accounts for more than one-third of global energy consumption and emissions. According to the International Energy Agency (IEA), building operations are responsible for 30 per cent of final energy consumption.[20] They are also linked to about 26 per cent of global energy-related emissions, of which 8 per cent are direct emissions and 18 per cent are indirect emissions from the production of electricity and heat used in buildings. While tracking the sector, the IEA found that in 2022, direct emissions from the buildings sector had fallen, although energy use in the building sector had risen by about 1 per cent.

Today, the number of carbon-neutral buildings—essentially buildings with net zero energy consumption or that have zero carbon emissions annually—has been steadily increasing. Many now operate using intelligent systems and renewable energy, and are off-the-grid or harvest energy onsite. Climate-sensitive design, backed by smart and integrated technology, minimize energy consumption through optimal use of light, heat and ventilation sources. Advanced, energy-efficient building technologies, backed by stricter building energy codes, will play an important role in helping cities shift towards becoming zero carbon.

The Net Zero Carbon Buildings Commitment, launched in 2018, advocates halving carbon emissions (including both operational and embodied) in the building/construction sector by 2030, and total decarbonization of the sector by 2050.[21] The Commitment currently has 175 signatories, including twenty-nine leading cities from across the world ranging from London, New York, Paris, Oslo and Helsinki to Johannesburg, San Francisco, Sydney, Medellín and Montreal.

According to a report[22] by the World Green Building Council (World GBC), which mooted the Net Zero Carbon Buildings Commitment, net zero buildings—both commercial and residential—currently comprise a paltry 1 per cent of all buildings worldwide.

But change is coming. There is now a growing list of buildings like the Venus and The Forge, Powerhouse Telemark (Norway), the Floating Office (Rotterdam), the No Footprint House (Costa

Rica) that claim to be net zero. In 2020, McDonald's opened its first net-zero energy restaurant, entirely powered by solar energy (your Big Mac cooked courtesy the sun, anyone?) at Disney World Resorts in Florida. Another example is the Unisphere. Completed 2018 and located in Maryland, (US), the Unisphere—conceived as a sustainable, net-zero–energy office for a pharmaceutical company, United Therapeutics—is often referred to as one of the world's largest net-zero–energy building. From nearly 3,000 solar panels that generate renewable, clean energy onsite, an 'energy wheel' that tracks energy consumption in real time, and thermal pool for temperature regulation, the building is designed to be net zero.

In December 2021, US President Biden signed his Executive Order on Catalyzing Clean Energy Industries and Jobs through Federal Sustainability, wherein the federal government was directed to use its procurement power to limit GHG. The executive order had a five-point agenda. Among the points were 'Net zero emissions from federal procurement no later than 2050, including a Buy Clean policy to promote use of construction materials with lower embodied emissions' and 'a net zero emissions building portfolio by 2045, including a 50 percent emissions reduction by 2032'. Indeed, government-backed initiatives have become increasingly important considering buildings rank among the largest energy consumers in the US, more than even transport and industry, accounting for almost 40 per cent of primary energy usage.[23] It follows in line with the US Department of Energy's Net-Zero Energy Commercial Building Initiative (CBI) that requires all commercial buildings in the country to be carbon neutral by 2050.

Waste

There's a day to celebrate mothers, fathers, love, the environment, water, population, blood donors, bicycles, women, refugees … So why has it taken so long to have a special day dedicated to waste? Finally, in a long-overdue gesture, we got an international day to mark Zero Waste in 2023: so go ahead, don't waste time on penciling in 30 March as International Zero Waste Day!

According to the UN, over 2.24 billion tons of municipal solid waste is generated every year. Tellingly, only slightly over half reaches managed waste facilities. More than three quarters of electronic waste is not safely disposed. Adding to this, 14 million tons of plastic waste is released into fragile marine ecosystems. UNEP states that the equivalent of one garbage truck of plastic is dumped into the ocean every minute.[24]

The Zero Waste Alliance inspired by its rather alliterative motto of 'working towards a world without waste', defines zero waste as 'the conservation of all resources by means of responsible production, consumption, reuse and recovery of products, packaging, and materials without burning and with no discharges to land, water or air that threaten the environment or human health.'

Similarly, the UN's zero waste approach embraces 'responsible production, consumption and disposal of products in a closed, circular system. This means that resources are reused or recovered as much as possible and that we minimize the pollution to air, land or water.'

Almost a decade ago, the European Union's European Pathway to Zero Waste (EPOW) programme[25] focused on sustainable utilization of resources through 4Rs, namely, reduce, recycle, reuse and recover. Funded by Life+, the financial arm of the EU, its projects in southeastern England aimed at achieving zero waste, setting the foundations for a 'recycling society' and establishing benchmarks for the rest of the EU to emulate.

Such governmental support continues in various forms across the world, with a host of non-state actors also attempting to mobilize action in private and public spheres. It recognizes that zero waste is a vast and complex terrain with multiple interlinked aspects. In 2020, for instance, Amsterdam declared itself the first city in the world to commit to building a circular economy, focusing on food and organic waste streams, consumer goods and the built environment.[26]

Overarchingly, innovating-to-zero solutions based on reduce, reuse, repair and recycle aim at generating less waste across a product's life cycle to advance sustainable development. In addition, initiatives cover extended producer responsibility and redesign, downcycling, composting, generating waste-based energy, and reducing waste and consumption in packaging, and targeting energy and resource rationalization. In time, such concepts of circularity envision a cradle-to-cradle ideal of complete recyclability.

Companies like Procter & Gamble have implemented innovative waste diversion strategies, such as turning toilet paper scraps into affordable roofing materials. The company aims to achieve 100 per cent recyclable or reusable packaging by 2030. Unilever, meanwhile, reached its zero-waste-to-landfill goal in 2016, six years ahead of schedule, across 242 factories in sixty-seven countries. Their innovations include transforming tea waste into textile dyes and using sludge to feed earthworms, which has saved over $225 million, while supporting employment generation. Unilever targets fully sustainable packaging by 2025.[27]

As is now becoming increasingly clear, zero waste has expanded well beyond basic waste-reduction measures for a single economic unit to embrace buildings, entire communities and cities.

As a child, I was always told how privileged I was to have food on the table every day. So, for me, the concept of zero waste has other implications. Consider that over 900 million tons of food is either lost or wasted every year.[28] The rather telling anecdote here is that if food loss and waste were a country, it would have the dubious distinction of being the third largest source of GHG emissions.[29] Or that food waste disposed in landfills generates 8 to 10 per cent of global GHG emissions. For me, innovating to zero here would mean not just food security but beyond that zero hunger and zero malnutrition.

I am convinced that we have the capacity, through innovation and ingenuity, to reduce waste in all its forms to truly zero.

Work

The pandemic marked a turning point for the concept of zero work. And by that, I certainly wasn't referring to zero volumes, time or attention spent on work. On the contrary, I think we all worked harder and, more importantly, smarter than we ever did. No, what I am referring to are the positive zeros. Initiatives which, for the most part, could result in safer, more flexible and efficient work environments.

The most obvious innovating to zero at the workplace are zero papers and zero emails. But how about the others like zero downtime, zero delays in delivery, zero client complaints and zero waiting time? And what about zero latency, zero-hour contracts and zero business-incubation period?

Zero Paper

Let us begin with zero paper, that is, a paperless office, as we move online. Quite frankly, an office with paper has become obsolete; I mean, when was the last time you stood near the office printer waiting patiently for it to spew out a cascade of paper? (And, somewhere out there, I hear a tree hollering out its thanks.)

Zero Emails

On the flip side, zero papers meant a deluge of emails. According to Statista, an astounding 333 billion emails were sent daily in 2022, with this figure set to climb to 392.5 billion by 2026. Little wonder then that a February 2021 study conducted by US-based email app company, Superhuman, of 1,000 US-based remote workers, identified work communications, such as emails or Microsoft Teams, as the biggest source of distraction on a daily basis and that, indeed, nearly two in three remote workers would prefer the tedium of an office commute if only to escape from the burden of dealing with the emails that pile up when working remotely.[30]

To me, innovating to zero here means two things. One, from a more limited perspective, is the idea of a zero inbox. A four-step process advocated by productivity specialist The Inbox Zero guy, Merlin Mann, exhorts people to delete, delegate, defer, or do it to get to a Zero Inbox. I better burst your bubble of happiness quickly, though. The zero here isn't a reference to the volume of messages in your inbox, but 'the amount of time an employee's brain is in his inbox.'[31]

The second, more broad-ranging approach is to go fully zero email. Most famously, of course, French IT services firm Atos Origin mooted this idea in 2011, with the aim of becoming a zero-mail company by 2014. Cited as reasons behind this decision were the constant distractions, lowered productivity and stress related to coping with a full-to-overflowing email inbox. The policy sought to eliminate internal emails and replace it with innovative enterprise socially collaborative software.

In my own case, I find I am organically reducing my dependence on emails. I am turning towards new communications apps like WhatsApp and Telegram that I find more convenient, nudging my email account towards redundancy. It allows me greater control over my work communications, reduces my distractions (my favorite command is 'mute notifications') and immeasurably enhances my productivity. Cloud-based tools, meanwhile, are raising the question of whether we really need an email system in the modern world? Probably not and that could save us the anguish of coming back to work from a holiday safe in the knowledge that we had zero inboxes.

A Best Practices Case Study

Atos: Zero Emails

I started my career in 1993 working for a government organization in India when most, if not all, internal communications were either handwritten or typewritten. Twice a day, every day, a flurry of files would find their way to my desk, which I would then have to plow through, sort, review and, finally, act upon. When emails burst onto the scene as a new means of office communication, I was excited, and appreciated the efficiency improvements that they promised.

Since those early days of email over three decades ago, a lot has changed: excitement has given way to drudgery, efficiency to a sense of being overwhelmed. We have become slaves to our inbox. On a typical day, I review over 250 emails, with only about 15 per cent relevant. I check emails from 7 a.m. until midnight, on weekends, in the bathroom, in the car or train, while waiting at airports, and even squeeze in a quick look during television commercial breaks. And yet, somehow, I seem unable to make even the slightest dent. My desperate efforts to keep up usually fail as colleagues and clients invariably expect me to respond in zero time. I am officially suffering from what I call 'email exhaustion'. I am sure that when MIT graduate Ray Tomlinson sent the world's first email in 1971 from one computer to another that was just a metre away, he did not anticipate his creation would have such dramatic ripple effects.

Zero emails is an innovating-to-zero concept that has gained popularity in the work environment over the last decade. The aim of any zero-email initiative is not so much to reduce communication as it is to enhance and improve enterprise communication. Through the use of innovative and efficient media and communication tools, employees using a variety of devices can work easily and productively from anywhere, everywhere, at any time.

According to Duchenaut and Watts,[32] email functions can be perceived in three ways: as a filing cabinet, a production line and a communication genre. When one adopts a zero-email strategy, one might wonder how the multiple functions described earlier can still be maintained. To illustrate, Atos S.E., Europe's largest IT services firm, explored an intriguing alternative when it adopted its zero-email policy in February 2011. Using new collaboration and social media tools that completely replaced all email communication, it hoped to fully achieve its zero-email target by 2013 for all internal communication purposes. Through this initiative, Atos S.E. aimed to promote social wellbeing, boost productivity, create sustainable business and spur greater innovation for its clients, while simultaneously reinventing its work environment and processes.

To achieve its zero-email target, Atos deployed a toolset that included a microblogging platform called Yammer, an online mindmapping tool called Mindmeister, an enterprise wiki, and a document management system. This set of tools was designed to help with communication, project management and collaboration, community writing, and even review and approval processes. Atos also envisaged the use of Enterprise 2.0, an enterprise social network that would integrate all the functions of the tools described earlier, to eventually replace all electronic mail by 2013.

For the function of filing and documentation, the Enterprise 2.0 platform was developed to enable the creation of group communities that would act as a repository of all files and communication. It was aimed at facilitating employee access to all information, with collaborative filtering features that would help them locate a particular file or data. For production lines or project management, the Enterprise 2.0 solution was expected to transform all email communication into signals using data mashups. Additionally, the wiki interface was conceived to simplify employee communication through a social-networking platform with 'updates' related to project alerts, peer-reviewed reports and collaborative project management, among others, from various team members. For the final function of emails covering communication, microblogging and discussion forums, Enterprise 2.0 platforms were meant to completely eliminate the need for communicating using email.

For Atos, the goal was not merely to become a zero-email company. It was also to improve processes in that journey and to accurately identify and overcome the restraints linked to email overload.

Although Atos failed to meet its zero-email target by the end of 2013, a study conducted by an independent firm in 2014 showed that the company had certified over 220 programmes as zero email and had slashed overall emails by 60 per cent.[33] This reduction was also good for the company's balance sheet as Atos' operating margin increased from 6.5 per cent to 7.5 per cent in 2013, with earnings rising by 50 per cent, although it was hard to prove (or disprove, as the case may be) that such gains were the direct result of employees not getting bogged down on their machines.

Atos's vision of zero emails is a promising start. However, if my continually deluged inbox is any indication, then a more comprehensive embrace of streamlined, paperless processes is still some distance away and will require significant cultural and technological shifts. This point was more tellingly highlighted when I visited a government office in India in early 2024. I felt quite nostalgic as my eyes followed a ubiquitous mountain of files wending their way across the office from one desk to another.

Zero Latency

Consider zero latency, which is, in many ways, an extension of our modern-day, on-demand culture. The need for instantaneous data retrieval at work will see the growing appeal of concepts of zero latency in the corporate world, in which the time lag between the receipt of and response to critical information is eliminated. This trend is being made possible by advanced connectivity technologies like 5G and 6G. By combining cellular and space technology, 6G will provide a fully connected anytime, anywhere, everywhere experience in the future. Such zero latency will be crucial for the autonomous world, especially for autonomous cars. More generally, a zero-latent world will be a game changer for our future.

Zero latency, in turn, is setting the stage for zero turnaround time where business decisions and processes can be made faster and, perhaps, even happen in real time.

Zero-Hours Contract

I remember interviewing Dr Jan Gupta, now president of Akkodis, a global smart-tech engineering company, in early 2021. Speaking about tech consulting and talent, he said that there had been a fundamental shift in the way young people thought about jobs and careers. For them, a job was about being challenged; they wanted to tackle a project for a couple of years, see its impact and then move onto something new, different and exciting. All of which made me feel positively Jurassic. After all, I worked almost two decades for one company. But I understood what Jan was saying: it is the age of the gig economy, and the idea of a zero-hours contract aligns with it.

Already a widely accepted, albeit controversial, concept in the workplace, it marks the intersection of advancing technology, evolving social demographics and changing business demands. Younger workforces want different types of flexible work environments, and a zero-hours contract affords just that. This kind of contract allows for flexible, on-demand employment, an arrangement that suits both employer and employee. No more of the stifling concept of working eight hours, five days a week. The UK government states that a zero-hours contract, or 'on call' work, means workers are on call to work when employers need them; employers do not have to give them work and employees do not have to do work when asked.[34] It's really the rise of the gig economy.

Across private and public, commercial to non-profit, banks to retail, leisure to tourism sectors, the idea of flexible, 'as and when' working has been widely used. Interestingly, while such employment practices were widely adopted in some countries like the UK—at one point, everyone from the country's largest sporting goods retailer, Sports Direct, to pharmaceutical giant, Boots, the NHS to the National Trust was using zero-hours contracts—other countries like New Zealand banned such contracts in 2016, citing them as being unfair and exploitative.

The Other Zeros

Some less contentious innovating-to-zero ideas at the workplace include leveraging advanced technologies to create, implement and commercialize business ideas in zero time. Here, go-to-market pressures will be alleviated by zero-time business incubation (ZTBI). This will see new types of cutting-edge infrastructure, IT and professional services that would enable ideas to be converted into strategy implementation and, perhaps, even new products or businesses in zero time. ZTBI will see tools such as online networking interfaces, file-sharing, instant market research and a host of other zero-related trends, such as zero management gaps, zero processing time and zero learning gaps.

Other zero ideas within the context of the workplace include zero friction capital—finding capital and optimizing its use; zero friction career—streamlining the movement of human capital between and within organizations so that their skills are optimally matched to current organizational needs; and zero friction education—creating a fluid system of work and education which allows people to move organically between both spheres while maximizing results at both professional and personal levels.

Zero work accidents

The concept of zero accidents or zero occupational hazards is geared towards ensuring the health, safety and wellbeing of employees in various workplace environments. Best practices stem from the premise that accidents are preventable, and use a combination of technology, training, commitment from leadership, active involvement of workers, a culture of safety, improved communication, and cooperation strategies to realize occupational safety and health (OSH).

General Electric, for instance, has a well-established environment, health and safety (EHS) policy. Shell has a Goal Zero, a 'no harm' initiative where it seeks to achieve effective operations alongside zero fatalities, zero accidents and zero significant incidents. It seeks to realize this goal by focusing on three key areas which it has identified as being high risk: personal, process and transport. The company claims that in 2021–22, the number of serious injuries and fatalities decreased from thirty-two to eight, and the number of serious injuries and fatalities per 100 million working hours (SIF-F) from 6.9 to 1.7.[35]

Zero Tolerance

In the age of #MeToo, zero-tolerance policies are an important concept, which can prevent inappropriate behaviour in the workplace. Proven to be successful in many organizations, these policies keep a check on harassment, discipline and even quality-control issues in the workplace.

Table 2.2: Zero in Work		
Zero papers	Zero-friction career	Zero-based scheduling
Zero emails	Zero-friction capital	Zero-based product development
Zero downtime	Zero-friction education	Zero-based hiring
Zero delays in delivery	Zero tolerance for discrimination	Zero-overtime policy
Zero client complaints	Zero defects	Zero-based leadership
Zero waiting time	Zero-based budgeting	Zero-error culture
Zero contract hours	Zero-cost marketing	Zero-confusion communication
Zero work accidents	Zero lateness	Zero-based performance review
Zero latency	Zero-hour workweek	Zero-interest loans
Zero business-incubation period	Zero-trust security model	Zero-hour crisis response
Zero-time business incubation	Zero overhead	Zero-based marketing

Cities

According to the World Economic Forum (WEF), while cities account for only around 3 per cent of the earth's land surface, they account for more than two-thirds of global carbon emissions.[36] Rapid urbanization and development imperatives have meant higher energy consumption. The key here is to address the challenges that come with spiraling energy demands, while finding sustainable ways to transition towards a net-zero future.

Today, more than 140 countries who contribute to over 90 per cent of GHG emissions have either already proposed or have established net-zero targets for 2050. By the end of 2022, eight countries declared that they had achieved net-zero emissions: Suriname, Guyana, Comoros, Bhutan, Gabon, Madagascar, Nieu (a self-governing state in free association with New Zealand) and Panama.[37]

At the G20 Summit held in September 2023 in New Delhi, India, G20 leaders pledged to achieve global net-zero emissions by around 2050, depending on their respective national circumstances. The mandate here was 'clean', 'efficient solutions' and 'zero and low carbon'.

Several cities, in the meantime, have committed to becoming carbon neutral—where the net carbon emissions generated annually by a city is absolutely zero. Worldwide, over 1,000 cities have committed to the UN's Cities Race to Zero initiative, part of the foundational United Nations Framework Convention on Climate Change (UNFCC)-led 'Race to Zero', which seeks to achieve a net-zero future by 2050.[38]

In April 2022, the European Commission revealed a list of 112 cities as part of the Cities Mission, an EU-led mission to have 100 climate-neutral and smart cities drawn from thirty-five EU member states and associated states by 2030.[39] Selected cities ranged from the more well-known, like Heidelberg, Barcelona, Florence, Athens and Copenhagen, to the less familiar like Gabrovo (Bulgaria), Differdange (Luxembourg), Elbasan (Albania), Košice (Slovakia) and Liepāja (Latvia).

For cities looking to combine development and improved quality of life together with carbon-neutrality, Copenhagen has long been acclaimed as a 'green growth' leader. In 2012, it announced its intention of becoming carbon-neutral by 2025. Over 100 green initiatives were introduced, from creating the infrastructure to become a city of cyclists, providing incentives to recycle, shifting to sustainable energy sources like wind and solar energy, focusing on making buildings more energy efficient. Sustainable practices and enhanced quality-of-life measures were welded with economic growth and more widespread stakeholder involvement. It seemed the city was doing everything right. So, it came as a surprise when in August 2022, the city defaulted on its 2025 carbon-neutral target. Two factors were indicted in this setback: a reliance on untested technology and the lack of accountability and proper coordination among key stakeholders. But while the 2025 target is now not possible, city authorities seemed optimistic that the delay would only be by a year or two. In further cause for optimism, the Danish Ministry of Foreign Affairs stated the country as a whole would have reduced its CO_2 emissions by 70 per cent in 2030 and become carbon neutral as planned in 2050.

How to build a zero-vision strategy: A structured approach

In essence then, 'innovating to zero' manifests in multiple ways at multiple levels in multiple areas from cities to countries, cars to crime, buildings to bras, factories to food, health to hunger, and even the opera (historic East Sussex opera house Glyndebourne has pledged to halve its direct carbon emissions by 2030, and reach net zero by 2050) to oenophilia (raise a toast to California's Fetzer Vineyards, the world's first zero-waste certified wine company).

The question we need to ask ourselves is whether we can truly conceive of this aspirational vision translating into real-world products and services? Can we use it to inform business and corporate strategies? If so, how can businesses and society as a whole benefit? And, perhaps most importantly, in a profit-driven environment, can a compelling business case be made for implementing a zero-vision strategy?

For instance, did Indian FMCG Britannia benefit commercially from producing nutritious and affordable biscuits to achieve its goal of zero malnutrition (read all about it in chapter 9)? How about Nissan? Did the Japanese automaker reap gains from having spent more than $1 billion on developing new electric-car technology? And if it did—as we may well assume to have been the case since electric vehicles (EVs) are mainstream today—then what processes did they follow in their zero-vision quest (read case study in chapter 4)? What was their approach, what techniques did they use, and can these be replicated across every business so we can all realize an effective zero-vision strategy? As it transpired, Nissan, which was the first to launch a zero-emission electric car in the modern era, was left far behind in the electrification race by Tesla. Why did this happen? Where did Nissan go wrong in its strategy?

Over the next few chapters, we will explore examples from various fields where zero can play a disruptive role—be it among communities or corporates, in the context of social or business agendas, either today or in the future. We will then look at how we can go about designing, developing and delivering a zero-vision strategy, in chapter 10. By the end, I hope we will be able to identify the fundamental building blocks that go into successfully implementing such an approach.

For me, a zero-vision strategy has two sides: on the one side, it is about eliminating the wrongs, the evils, the negatives and, on the other, it is about championing the rights, the good, the positives.

It is about sparking sustainable innovation in environmental and economic spheres and being committed to balancing business and social imperatives. I find it a remarkably powerful concept that holds promise of alleviating massive social inequities and enhancing quality of life indices by tackling apparently intractable problems like pollution, poverty and violence, among others. I believe it can foster new paradigms that herald inclusive, sustainable, responsible growth. All very well, I know, in theory. But what about practice? How does one get around to the brasstacks of implementing this zero-vision in what is essentially a chaotic world full of contradictory pushes and pulls?

While I will delve into greater detail about my ten-step process to successfully achieve a zero-vision strategy in chapter 10, what I will emphasize here is the need for a clearly defined and structured approach. This is a prerequisite. It will begin with articulating what, why and how this vision is unique to you or your organization, what value you believe these new ideas can add and how they can impel your goals. For businesses, this will mean something as fundamental as identifying and understanding customer expectations and unmet market needs. Imagination, entrepreneurship, creativity, ingenuity, intelligence and endurance—without these attributes, any idea is bound to crash even before take-off. But equally, I will add, the virtue of pragmatism that will allow you to assess whether these ideas can be viably translated into real-world applications, what their potential impact might be, and how they might align with the big picture. Once the wheat has been separated from the chaff will come the stage of trialing prototypes/pilots in real-world scenarios and, subsequently, implementing only the most promising ones. At this stage, it will be critical to establish key performance indicators that track progress. The ability to scale successful implementations and continuously adapt, based on new insights and changing dynamics, will be pivotal for a zero vision to survive and thrive. And, finally, I will repeat that adage—you learn more from your failures than you do from your successes. Failures will be inevitable but if we see them as opportunities for learning, course correction and refining action, our march to zero vision will merely be delayed, not ended.

3

INNOVATING TO ZERO IN THE INDUSTRIAL SECTOR

Industry 5.0: Where Zero and Industry Converge

The discovery of molecules led to a better understanding of mechanical energy which, in turn, precipitated the first Industrial Revolution in the middle of the eighteenth century, from around 1750 to 1850. This breakthrough resulted in the world economy shifting from farming to industrial manufacturing, with machines replacing and limiting the need for human labour.

Then came the period between the 1850s and the 1940s, when we had the second Industrial Revolution. This was linked to the discovery of electrons in the early nineteenth century and a keener appreciation of the many applications of electrical energy. Indeed, for those who dismiss generative AI as hype, there are lessons to be learnt from this period. Progress was 'electrifying'—from Benjamin Franklin's observations on electricity to Michael Faraday's electric dynamo, from Alessandro Volta's battery to the highly charged slugfest between Nikola Tesla and Thomas Alva Edison to determine whether AC or DC current would be better

CHART 3.1 : EVOLUTION OF INDUSTRIAL REVOLUTIONS

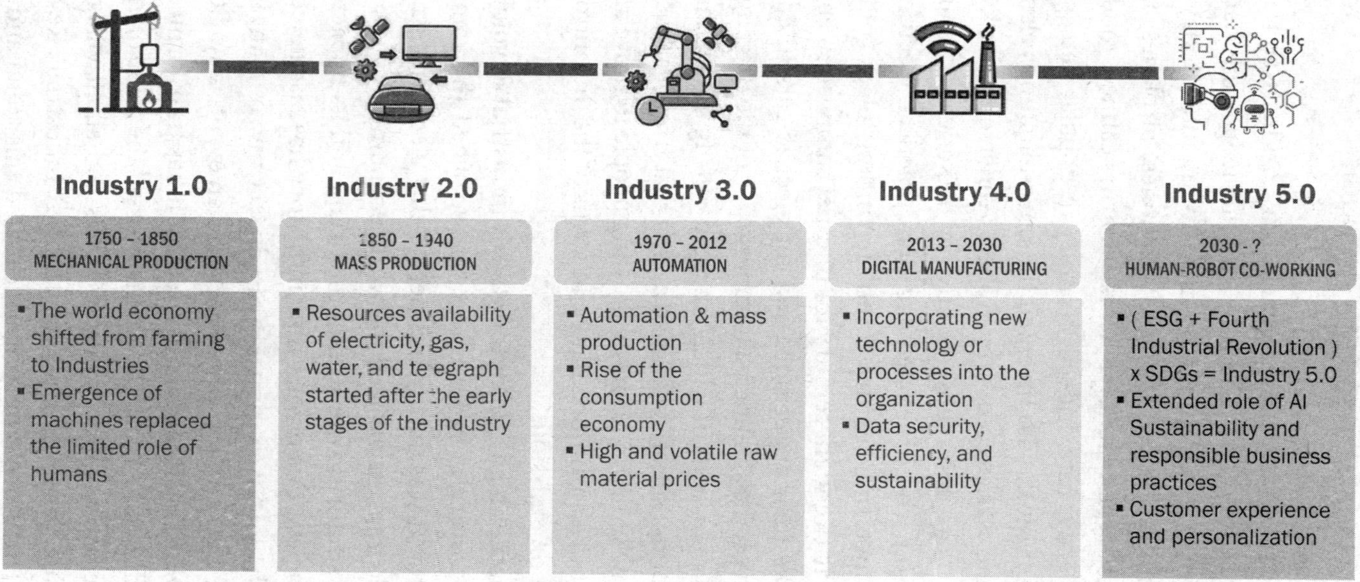

Source : Markets and Markets

suited for electric-power generation. Products and applications flew thick and fast. The leaps in knowledge laid the foundation for many of the things we take for granted today—batteries, light bulbs, electric motors, telephones, airplanes, fans, power stations, typewriters, cameras, aspirin, canned food, and, yes, even electric cars. Indeed, contrary to popular perception, it was not Elon Musk who invented the now ubiquitous electric vehicle (EV); he was preceded by Robert Anderson's clunky prototype electric car and, subsequently, by American chemist William Morrison who developed the first 'practical' electric car in the later nineteenth century. It took us finding 'black gold', aka oil, in the early twentieth century for internal combustion engines (ICE) to make their appearance and for electric cars to end up being parked on the sidelines. The emergence of the ICE engine and the automobile, both of which emerged during the second Industrial Revolution, set off a chain of events that irrevocably changed our lives—whether in terms of allowing people to move around more easily but also, unfortunately, in terms of the uncontrolled growth of carbon emissions.

Another highlight of the golden Industrial Revolution 2.0 was the discovery of radio waves that spawned the communication industry. It was during this period that electricity, gas, water and the telegraph galvanized the world economy.

As a futurist who studies the future and its impact on humans and society, this pivotal time in history has fascinated me for the long shadows it continues to cast. In fact, my company has a process called 'backcasting', where we study an event—say, COVID—and then work backwards to assess how it has transformed society.

Industrial Revolution 1.0 kickstarted the trend of urbanization. We began moving from rural areas and small villages to towns and, in time, cities. The second Industrial Revolution, or Industrial Revolution 2.0, accelerated this trend and was further propelled by the advent of the mass-produced Model T. In its two-decade production run, over 15 million of this game-changing vehicle were sold, with Henry Ford famously quipping, 'There's no use trying to pass a Ford, because there's always another one just ahead.' What Henry Ford did not realize was that he had just sparked a new trend, that is, 'mobility', which enabled the rapid, sustained growth of urbanization and its offshoot, sub-urbanization, characterized by smaller communities or residential areas developing adjacent to or within commuting distance of large towns and cities.

The period from the 1970s to around 2012 was characterized by the rise of automation and mass production. The third Industrial Revolution facilitated unprecedented productivity, enabling the mass production and ownership of consumer appliances and products. Households began accumulating copious amounts of goods, spurred by technological advancements and decreasing costs. It was the era of conspicuous consumption.

This period saw the expansion of industrial conglomerates like General Electric (led by the legendary 'neutron' Jack Welch) Johnson & Johnson, IBM and Siemens, which harnessed automation to dominate global markets. Companies transitioned from domestic to international and then global operations in their push for greater efficiency and lower production costs.

Offshore production became a hallmark of this period, significantly boosting the economies of Japan and Germany initially, and later China. These countries became global economic powerhouses, underlining the era's legacy of interdependent, interconnected and intertwined economies.

Several innovative zero concepts made their appearance during this time, most famously Toyota's zero-defects initiative that aimed for nothing less than perfection. Zero waste, zero errors, zero accidents in manufacturing, zero downtime, zero inventory (or the just-in-time production) were among the other popular innovating-to-zero concepts that gained appeal during this period. Table 3.1 shows all the zeros that can be adopted in the industrial world.

Table 3.1: Zero in the Industrial World		
Zero waste	Zero overproduction	Zero planned obsolescence
Zero emissions	Zero exposure	Zero-pollution manufacturing
Zero accidents	Zero-error production	Zero technology gaps
Zero defects	Zero cost overruns	Zero child labour
Zero downtime	Zero discrimination	Zero water scarcity
Zero inventory	Zero-water waste	Zero packaging waste
Zero-energy buildings	Zero-excess inventory	Zero-conflict sourcing
Zero deforestation	Zero discharge	Zero-leakage systems
Zero contamination	Zero planned maintenance	Zero-defect assembly
Zero noise	Zero grid dependency	Zero talent churn
Zero carbon	Zero counterfeit	Zero time to market
Zero plastic	Zero corruption	Zero innovation time
Zero-defect manufacturing	Zero residuals	Zero failures in innovation pipeline
Zero hazard	Zero-impact operations	Zero shrinkage
Zero corrosion	Zero overproduction	Zero design-to-shelves response time
		Zero-carbon products

Somewhere in the middle of the last decade, we entered—and are now in the midst of—what we call Industry 4.0. Marked by digital manufacturing, cyber-physical systems and intelligent computing, Industry 4.0 is described by leading German software company SAP as 'the integration of intelligent digital technologies into manufacturing and industrial processes. It encompasses a set of technologies that include industrial IoT networks, AI, Big Data, robotics, and automation. Industry 4.0 allows for smart manufacturing and the creation of intelligent factories. It aims to enhance productivity, efficiency and flexibility while enabling more intelligent decision-making and customization in manufacturing and supply chain operations.'

So, if the first Industrial Revolution was powered by steam energy, the second harnessed electricity and the third was driven by early automation and machinery, then Industry 4.0 represents an era of digital transformation propelled by disruptive trends such as the exponential growth of data and connectivity, sophisticated analytics, enhanced human–machine interaction, and major advancements in robotics. These elements are converging to integrate state-of-the-art technologies and processes into organizational structures, with a strong focus on data security, efficiency and sustainability.

Today, we find ourselves engaged with Industrial Revolution 4.0—an epoch that my friend Pranjal Sharma talks about in his book *The Next New: Navigating the Industrial Revolution*[1]—which will be remembered for the integration of technologies that are connected, interactive and intuitive. The end objective of this technological convergence will be to derive maximum cost, time and resource efficiencies in manufacturing, improve operational processes, and mitigate losses through the use of an arsenal of technologies—5G, IoT, AI, robotics, analytics, cloud and industrial platforms, among them—in forecasting, transportation, logistics, predictive maintenance, inventory optimization, cycle-time reduction and supply-chain optimization.

Going by this, you've probably already guessed that I am heading in the direction of what MarketsandMarkets as well as Meta term the 'Industrial Metaverse'. MarketsandMarkets forecasts this industry to be worth $400 billion by 2028, growing at a CAGR of 43 per cent. In the future, the Industrial Metaverse will include AR/VR, digital twins that blur the lines between the physical and digital worlds, and advanced 3D printing.

Industry 4.0 will necessitate a major shift in business models with companies like Siemens, ABB and Schneider, among others, moving to platform-as-a-service business models as opposed to selling factory automation equipment on a CAPEX basis. In future, operation technology (OT), information technology (IT), engineering design data (ET) and the industrial internet of things (IIoT) will be integrated into these models, across both discrete and process industries. As a consequence, zero CAPEX-based models will burgeon.

Some of the zero initiatives introduced during the previous Industrial Revolution 3.0 have been the focus of sustained efforts by corporates and governments in the Industrial Revolution 4.0 period. These objectives continue to garner attention with the advantage of hindsight, particularly with the realization that we have, perhaps, gone too far in our quest for profits at all costs. Accordingly, organizations have not only adopted the more obvious zero goals of reducing carbon emissions but, equally, have concentrated on championing a multitude of zero goals with beneficial societal impacts like zero child labour, zero deforestation, zero discharge and zero pollution. Many organizations have gone even further, committing to carbon-neutral goals, with most large companies establishing clear roadmaps to achieve carbon neutrality between 2030 and 2050. Of course, one could argue that this might be a case of too slow and too late and whether more can and, indeed, should be done by embedding sustainable 'zero' concepts across organizational DNA. It remains to be seen whether good intent will translate into action.

Meanwhile, sometime before the end of this decade, we will see the shift to Industry 5.0 which the EU describes as 'a vision of industry that aims beyond efficiency and productivity as the sole goals and reinforces the role and the contribution of industry to society'.

This marks an important departure from the EU's approach to Industry 4.0, since 'it places the wellbeing of the worker at the center of the production process and uses new technologies to provide prosperity beyond jobs and growth while respecting the production limits of the planet'.

In his book, Pranjal avers that social impact considerations were not always a factor during Industrial Revolution 4.0. With its focus on social wellbeing, therefore, Industrial Revolution 5.0 represents an improvement on the 4.0 version. According to him, the additional objectives ingrained in the current Industrial Revolution are sustainability, governance and social impact. He notes that the technological solutions that underpin Industrial Revolution 5.0 account for the impacts of social inclusion, environmental sustainability and enhanced accountability, while embracing an element of humanity—people over profits, as it were—by the industrial world.

If the Fifth Industrial Revolution were to be represented as a mathematical equation, Pranjal says, this is how it would look:

(ESG + fourth industrial revolution) × SDGs = Industry 5.0

He summarizes the key pillars of the fifth Industrial Revolution as:

- Technological breakthroughs: Rise of AI, material science, new fuels, among others

- Values, ethics, safety and social equity: Increased governance with a focus on social inclusion
- Climate-change goals and accountability: Tech will be expected to serve the objective of sustainability and accountability of action.

Industry 5.0's future envisages enhanced roles for robots and AI in manufacturing, including closer collaboration between humans and robots. This will mark a major change from the previous Industrial Revolutions which invariably placed humans in the middle of all manufacturing processes.

Just as Industry 3.0 was about mass production and Industry 4.0 about customization, Industry 5.0 will be about hyper personalization and realizing a meaningful customer experience. It, consequently, underscores the need for zero-vision approaches to be augmented from the design stage to the retail-shelf stage, for continuous innovation (or zero time to innovation) and for zero complaints—all propelling the quest for customer satisfaction.

Also, just as Industry 4.0 was technology-driven, focused on automation and the use of technology, Industry 5.0 is expected to be value-driven, reinforcing the spotlight on people. Human wellbeing will be at its core, spurred by a combination of technology, carbon neutrality, and zero-vision goals that promote societal benefits.

A Best-Practices Case Study
General Motors: Factory ZERO

With the launch of Factory ZERO, General Motors (GM) stepped on the accelerator towards an all-electric future. Inaugurated in November 2021, this cutting-edge assembly plant located in Michigan (US) stands testament to GM's vision of a world with zero crashes, zero emissions and zero congestion. Formerly known as the Detroit-Hamtramck plant, Factory ZERO has been reborn as GM's first fully dedicated electric vehicle (EV) assembly plant, signalling a new era in automotive manufacturing.[2]

The factory's new name isn't merely a rebranding exercise. Since 1985, the Detroit-Hamtramck plant churned out over three million vehicles, but today, the state-of-the-art Factory ZERO is dedicated to producing multiple electric brands, including the GMC Hummer EV SUV, Hummer EV Pickup, Chevy Silverado EV and GMC Sierra EV with the 2025 Cadillac Escalade IQ set for production later this year.[3]

Sustainability and Innovation at Every Step

GM has equipped the plant with advanced technology and tooling to ensure it aligns with the company's broader commitment to sustainability. The factory will be powered entirely by renewable energy, thanks to DTE Energy's solar installations, including a 30 kilowatt solar carport and a 516 kilowatt solar array. By 2030, GM aims to power all its US facilities with renewable energy, and Factory ZERO is leading the way.

But the commitment to sustainability goes even deeper. During the plant's transformation, GM took an eco-friendly approach, repurposing concrete waste from the old facility to create temporary roadways around the site. This focus on sustainability extends beyond the factory walls, as Factory ZERO also features a certified 16.5 acre wildlife habitat that attracts monarch butterflies and even the occasional wild turkey.

The facility is a showcase for sophisticated manufacturing, leveraging the latest in internet-of-things (IoT) technology to enhance both safety and efficiency. The plant is teeming with connected devices, from sensors to robotics, all of which play a crucial role in ensuring the highest quality in the production process. Among the many innovations at Factory ZERO is the installation of Verizon's 5G Ultra-Wideband technology, making it the first US automotive plant to embrace this next-generation wireless network. With 5G, the factory can manage thousands of devices simultaneously, supporting everything from automated guided vehicles that shuttle materials around the plant to the latest emerging technologies that will shape the future of manufacturing.

GM has committed a staggering $35 billion to the development of electric and autonomous vehicles, with plans to launch thirty EV models globally by 2025. By 2035, it aims to offer an all-electric light-vehicle lineup, and Factory ZERO is the flagship of this ambitious strategy.

A Commitment to a Cleaner World

The plant is a critical component of the company's plan to eliminate tailpipe emissions from new light-duty vehicles by 2035 and achieve carbon neutrality across its global products and operations by 2040. Through innovative practices like recycling stormwater for use in cooling towers and the fire-suppression system, and repurposing materials from the plant's renovation, GM is proving that sustainability is a workable business model.

With every EV that rolls off the assembly-line Factory ZERO, GM is not just keeping pace with the future of mobility, they're driving it.

At this stage, much of this is still theory. And the businessman who will build a factory from purely altruistic, zero-vision motives is a myth. Nevertheless, innovating to zero holds promise to be the versatile hero of the industrial sector. Indeed, as seen from the earlier table, a first cut of zero-concept examples in the industrial sector yielded over a hundred (and counting) zero interest-rate policies to zero inflation, zero risk investment to zero interest financing, zero-based leasing to zero- based inventory, zero-based auditing to zero-based business models—possibilities.

Perhaps, a combination of carrot (that is, cheaper and abundant renewables rather than fossil fuels) and stick (for example, strict emission penalties) could be the spark that lights up Industry 5.0, an era that will be imbued with a sprawling, magnificently ambitious and, most importantly, attainable zero vision.

4

INNOVATING TO ZERO IN THE AUTOMOTIVE SECTOR

The automotive industry has long grappled with what I refer to as three core 'evils'. The first is traffic accidents, which claim over 1.3 million lives annually. The second is pollution, with transport-related emissions posing significant health risks. The third is congestion, where prolonged traffic jams elevate stress levels. To these, I would add a fourth challenge: zero growth. The industry has witnessed little growth in recent years, with annual vehicle production hovering below 90 million, far short of the 100 million target in global sales.

The First Evil: Zero Accidents, Zero Deaths

Over two decades ago, Sweden introduced a groundbreaking initiative called Vision Zero, aiming to eliminate serious injuries and deaths from traffic accidents, with an ambitious goal of achieving zero fatalities by 2050. This initiative has inspired similar programmes across North America and Europe, yielding promising results.

Automakers have followed suit with Mercedes-Benz, Toyota, General Motors (GM), and Volvo among the many that are already making significant strides towards the vision of zero accidents. Such efforts have been supported by collaborations between technology developers, infrastructure planners and policymakers, all working to enhance vehicle and road safety.

Swedish automaker Volvo, for instance, pledged that no one would die in a new Volvo vehicle after its 2020 models hit the road. This goal has not been fully realized with Volvo attributing many of these incidents to impaired driving. To address this, Volvo is turning to in-car cameras equipped with AI to detect distracted or intoxicated drivers and intervene to prevent them from operating the vehicle, thereby protecting both the driver and others on the road.[1]

Similarly, leading suppliers in the automotive sector have embraced the zero-accident philosophy. Continental Automotive Systems, a key provider of driver assistance and safety technologies, has committed to accident-free driving through its vision-zero strategy. This strategy employs both passive safety systems, such as airbags and seatbelts, which mitigate injury after an accident, and active safety technologies, such as anti-lock braking systems (ABS), Electronic Stability Control (ESC) and driver monitoring systems (DMS), which aim to prevent accidents from occurring in the first place.

Is it possible to eliminate car accidents entirely? The answer lies in the future, but the groundwork for zero fatalities is being laid today. We have already made significant progress using a combination of active safety features like ABS, ESC and advanced driver assistance systems (ADAS), such as Volvo's collision-avoidance systems. The rise of autonomous vehicles, particularly Level 3 and Level 4 autonomous systems, will further advance this goal. And even if accidents do occur, passive safety systems, such as airbags, could potentially prevent fatalities altogether.

The Path to Full Autonomy

The transition to fully autonomous vehicles is advancing faster than one might expect. While it took nearly two centuries to move from mechanical systems to automation, the leap to Level 4 autonomy, where vehicles can operate independently in specific conditions, will likely be achieved in a quarter century. Level 5 autonomy, where vehicles can drive themselves entirely without human input, remains several decades away.

In the meantime, several factors are accelerating this shift towards autonomy. Demographic changes, such as an aging population, coupled with labour shortages and rising labour costs, are driving the demand for autonomous systems. As the workforce shrinks, the need for these systems to fill critical gaps has become more urgent. Technological advances in high-speed connectivity, sensing, processing capabilities and AI are also making it possible for autonomous vehicles to integrate seamlessly into everyday life.

By 2030, the market for Level 3 autonomous vehicles is projected to grow at a remarkable compound annual growth rate (CAGR) of 86 per cent, with over 6 million units expected on the road.[2] Level 4 autonomous vehicles will see more limited commercial growth, with around 1 million units projected by 2030. However, Level 5 vehicles are not expected to achieve widespread market penetration for quite some time.

In the coming years, OEMs will increasingly offer semi-autonomous features on a subscription basis, allowing customers to access advanced driving technologies on a monthly or annual basis. For Level 4 vehicles, ride-hailing services will likely dominate, with pricing based on distance travelled.

A Future without Fatalities

The day when we achieve zero fatalities in road accidents globally, including in developing countries, is within reach. If policymakers, industry leaders and technology innovators work together, I believe this goal can be realized within the next decade. Through continued advancements in vehicle-safety technologies, autonomous systems and collaboration between the public and private sectors, the vision of zero deaths on the road is no longer a distant dream.

The Second Evil: Zero Emissions

For both consumers and automakers, the environmental impact of transportation is staggering. According to the International Council on Clean Transportation (ICCT), light-duty vehicles—cars and trucks—are responsible for 40 per cent of transportation-related carbon emissions. To decarbonize the transport sector, 67 per cent to 90 per cent of passenger vehicles must be zero-emission by 2050.[3] Innovation in this area is advancing rapidly, with electric batteries, hydrogen-powered fuel cells and biofuels leading the charge toward achieving zero emissions.

This naturally brings us to Elon Musk and Tesla. Under Musk's leadership and vision for a sustainable future, Tesla has been at the forefront of energy innovation, developing high-performance, all-electric Zero Emission Vehicles (ZEVs). Tesla is also driving the transition to scalable clean-energy generation and storage solutions. Meanwhile, Chinese automaker BYD has emerged as a leader in the EV market. As of March 2022, BYD ceased internal combustion engine (ICE) vehicle production and now exclusively produces EVs. Additionally, BYD's global headquarters in China is a zero-carbon facility featuring numerous energy-efficient and environmentally friendly systems.

Other Chinese EV manufacturers, such as Nio, Li Auto, XPeng and Geely, have rapidly caught up with and, in some cases, even surpassed their Japanese counterparts, who were early advocates of emissions-free driving. Toyota's hybrid Prius and Nissan's all-electric Leaf have become legendary in the automotive world. Honda, for its part, is working to join Toyota and Hyundai in offering commercially available hydrogen-fuelled vehicles.

Today, nearly every automaker is focused on transitioning to ZEVs. Nissan aims to have 55 per cent of its sales come from EVs by 2030. Land Rover plans to go fully electric by 2036, while Jaguar has set an earlier target of 2025. Ford targets 600,000 battery-electric vehicle (BEV) sales by 2026, and Rolls Royce is committed to producing a fully electric lineup by 2030.

Toyota's Beyond Zero strategy takes a broader approach, aiming not only for zero emissions but also to add new value beyond it. The company is working to eliminate carbon emissions across its entire production process and product lineup. Toyota's portfolio of carbon-neutral vehicles includes Hybrid Electric Vehicles (HEVs), Plug-in Hybrid Electric Vehicles (PHEVs), Full Battery Electric Vehicles (BEVs) and Fuel Cell Electric Vehicles (FCEVs). In May 2021, Toyota became the first company to race a hydrogen-powered vehicle. Additionally, Toyota Metal, part of the Toyota Group, uses a design-to-dismantle approach to recover almost 400 tons of parts daily for reuse.

But when can we expect the automotive industry to achieve 100 per cent zero-emission vehicles? According to data (Chart 4.1) from MarketsandMarkets Automotive Group, this milestone is unlikely to occur for at least two more decades. By the end of this decade, EVs are expected to achieve about 30 per cent market penetration, surpassing ICE vehicles sometime in the mid-2030s.

CHART 4.1: BATTERY ELECTRIC VEHICLES SALES TIPPING POINT

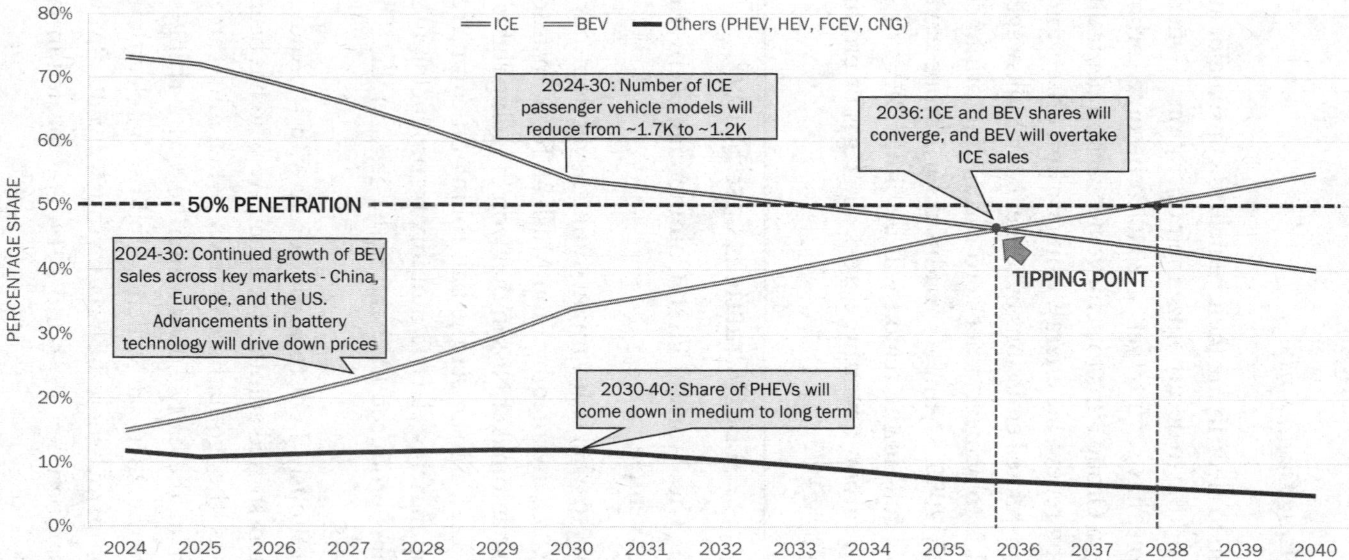

Source: MarketsandMarkets (MnM) Analysis, Desk Research, Discussions with experts

Decarbonizing Operations

In addition to electrifying their vehicle lineups, major automakers are also working to decarbonize their operations. General Motors, for example, has set a target of 2040 to become carbon-neutral. Volkswagen Group aims to achieve net carbon neutrality by 2030 by adopting renewable energy, using carbon offsets and reducing production-related emissions by 50 per cent. Volkswagen's longer-term goal is to achieve a net-zero carbon footprint across all its facilities by 2050. Hyundai's roadmap for Europe envisions that all vehicles sold in the region will be either BEVs or FCEVs by 2035, with carbon neutrality across all stages of production and operation by 2045.

A Best Practices Case Study

Nissan: The World's First Commercial, Zero Emission Electric Vehicle

Contrary to what many might think, the modern-day electric car was not invented by Elon Musk at Tesla. Instead, it was Japanese automaker Nissan that won bragging rights with its Nissan Leaf. Nissan set the ball rolling on commercializing and popularizing electric mobility by producing the world's first, mass produced EV, beating the Tesla Model S by about two years.

Fortuitously, I got to work closely with Dr Andy Palmer, the much-storied automotive executive who has been widely hailed as the 'godfather' of EVs, when our career paths crossed in the early 2000s when he was a rising star and then in the 2020s at Switch Mobility, the electric bus and van company, where he was my boss. Eventually, as COO of Nissan between 1991 and 2014, and located in Japan for the final thirteen years, Andy was seen as being the driving force behind the successful development of the Nissan Leaf and eNV200.

So who better to interview about innovating to zero than Andy? To understand why the Nissan Leaf was conceived and how Nissan became the first major OEM to launch a product that became a springboard for EVs, aka ZEV, globally.

It wasn't so much altruistic spirit as much as a competitive streak that birthed the zero-emission Nissan Leaf. As Andy says, 'I wish I could tell you that the Leaf was launched in the first instance to save the world—it wasn't. It was developed to mitigate the challenge posed by Toyota, which was kicking our backsides with the Prius! Setting aside this somewhat prosaic motivation, what the Leaf ended up achieving—a breakthrough ZEV—was quite inspiring.' That's one of the things I have long admired about Andy, the fact that he's always been a straight talker.

Wind back to 1997 when Toyota launched the world's first full hybrid car, the Toyota Prius. By the early 2000s, it had become a runaway bestseller. Honda followed in November 1999 with a mild hybrid offering—the Insight—that looked very much like it had been driven right off a Hollywood sci-fi movie set. This left Nissan in a dilemma—should it develop another hybrid competitor or aim for something completely different?

The hour maketh the man. In 2002, Nissan's CEO, Carlos Ghosn tapped company insider and rising star, Andy Palmer, to move to company headquarters in Japan. From his initial role as programme director for light commercial vehicles, Andy would go on to head product planning, corporate planning and sales and marketing. No sooner had he stepped into the dohyōthan that his sales and marketing team began haranguing him for a C-segment hybrid to neutralize their two Japanese rivals. Toyota was winning the battle of the C-segment vehicles—tellingly, the vehicle segment that accounts for the largest volume of car sales, globally.

But Andy was adamant that he did not want to create another competitor to the Prius (what's the fun in being a follower?) and had to fight some skunk projects that were working secretly to develop hybrid vehicles. Luckily for him, back in 2001, Carlos Ghosn had created a new organizational structure with six new programme directors. These programme directors, also referred to as vehicle-line directors, functioned like Daimyos, or mini CEOs, within Nissan. They were tasked with controlling budgets and P&Ls of the vehicle lineup that they managed and were responsible for the success of their vehicle portfolios. Interestingly, the floundering commercial vehicles division was missing a programme director. In stepped Andy to himself try and fix the slide. Within this division was another loss-making product—the Californian Compliance Vehicle called the Nissan Altra EV, an export-only electric version of an EV that Nissan had previously developed explicitly to meet California emission needs. What the Altra did was give Andy an all-access pass to Nissan's state-of-the-art, advanced R&D centre team that was working on electrification of vehicles. It allowed him to get an in-depth look at the battery capability that was being developed and win the support of the head of R&D, who rose to the challenge of developing a full BEV as opposed to a passive 'me too' strategy of developing yet another Prius fighter.

Importantly, Andy also managed to get, as he terms it, vital 'air cover' by convincing Carlos Ghosn to back him.

Carlos supported the product even as it racked up losses with a sales price barely covering the cost of the BOM.

It was not easy to convert this vision to reality, as Andy explains. There was considerable internal resistance from all three regional heads and the CFO, and external pressure too.

One big challenge was finding automotive suppliers that could offer car-grade battery and other electrical components. To make the battery, Nissan approached NEC and, subsequently, created a joint venture called AESC, in partnership with NEC Corporation. It was a difficult task for Nissan to convince its JV partners seeing as it was that it had never built car-size lithium-ion batteries and that its interest lay mainly in anode and cathode materials, rather than the cells themselves. Nissan also had to convince its French partner, Renault, about the viability of this plan. But, as is clear in hindsight, cooperation between the two companies was lukewarm, at best. Renault was working on its own model, the Zoe. The plan had been to develop a synergetic platform, but the two companies ultimately ended up sharing only one connector.

The development of an EV marked a major shift in product development. It required Nissan to undertake huge customer and market studies to understand how people used their cars, what load they carried, how many miles they drove daily, how many journeys they did every day, where they parked, whether they had a one-phase or three-phase electrical connections in their homes, and much more, as all these parameters had an impact on the range and charging of the vehicle which then dictated the size of the battery.

It did not help that the batteries cost $1500 per KWH (today they are closer to $110 per KWH), which meant that a 30 KWH battery alone would cost more than the Toyota Prius. Andy and Nissan had a mission and that was to design a vehicle with a price point of around US$ 30,000. There were some brutal cost reduction plans with economies of scale across engineering and sourcing. Andy's way of working meant everyone had to sign off on the cost-reduction plan and adhere to it, something I have learnt while working with him. His so-called cost reductions, also termed 'haircuts', are brutal targets set to the engineering and supplier sourcing teams to brings costs in alignment with targets. Andy was an architect in Nissan, and then later in Switch Mobility. He had experience of setting up a department whose role was to reduce costs across the value chain.

There were also external challenges from industry naysayers, one of whom suggested to Nissan that it might as well dump both the $4 billion and the Nissan Leaf into the Pacific Ocean. It did not help that the Lehman Brothers crash in 2008 had its most profound impact on the auto industry, with the Big 3 in the US more or less going bankrupt, and Nissan itself facing liquidity issues. However, with adversity comes opportunity.

The banking crisis led to government bailouts on the condition that the funds be used to support green vehicles. Andy and his team in Nissan were aware and more than ready.

Then came the kinboshi moment—to overcome some of these internal and external challenges, and to steer clear from insider efforts to kill this project, Nissan created a separate division called the Zero Emission business unit. All functions—from R&D, product planning, sales and marketing, and others—were housed in this division. This was a master stroke—creating for the people working in this division what Andy terms a 'passion project'. The more the resistance externally, the more motivated the team became to make it a success and prove them wrong. In many big companies, divisions work in silos. Having this 'company-within-a-company' structure with all the departments under one roof strengthened collaboration in quest of a common goal. Nissan also created a special Customer Insights division and (rather unusually) brought in experts like psychologists, rather than engineers, to help the product development and planning teams understand customer behaviour so that they, in turn, could design the right vehicle characteristics.

Nissan very quickly realized that game changer though it was, their EV had its limitations in terms of driving range and needed an ecosystem play. This meant that they also needed a strong connectivity package to help customers find convenient charging points. So the ZEV became the test bed for Nissan to develop its future-connected car services. Andy recalls discussions—more like arguments—with Elon Musk on whether the connected car services should be developed in-house or, given the bandwidth issues he was facing, developed externally. I guess this is one area where Nissan perhaps lost out to Tesla, which managed to develop a fully connected car platform with advanced functionality like software over the air (SOTA) updates.

Interestingly, Nissan realized quite early on that what it was doing was much more than just competing with Toyota; it was creating a zero-emission vehicle that would have a profound impact on the planet in that this could be the first vehicle with a zero well-to-wheel footprint that could also be net zero carbon. Therefore, the vision expanded, and

Nissan started signing MOUs and setting up partnerships and alliances with energy providers, governments, recyclers and others to ensure the vehicle was measured on its well-to-wheel footprint.

What Nissan did not realize was that the launch of its first commercial ZEV would galvanize the entire organization, with Nissan entering a golden period from 2008 to 2015. At the time, Nissan was one of the first to come out with autonomous vehicle features and even debated debuting it on the Leaf before finally deciding against it, using the logic that there was enough (and more) disruption on show in the vehicle.

In 2012, heralded by the tagline 'Innovation that Excites', Nissan mounted an aggressive global campaign led by the Nissan Leaf. Nissan's brand went up several notches, even as growth in terms of volume and market share across all product lines and across all regions of the world increased strongly.

Nissan has since sold over 1 million EVs in over fifty countries. Today, EVs account for about 15 per cent of annual global car sales. By the end of 2030, this figure is poised to go up to 30 per cent with roughly 30 million EV units forecast to be sold annually in 2030. At this pace, EVs are projected to overtake ICE vehicles sometime by the middle of the next decade, as shown in Chart 4.1, as a plan to beat the competition, through a vision-zero strategy, Nissan has been able to change the face of mobility. In its quest to beat the competition, Nissan's vision-zero strategy didn't just win, it won big, rewriting the rules of automotive industry and in the process, the playbook for mobility's future as well.

The Third Evil: Congestion

As we all know from personal experience, one of the most frustrating aspects of driving is being stuck in traffic. On a recent trip to Mumbai, for example, I spent nearly five hours traveling just 30 kilometres across the city. This raises the question: Can the automotive industry and policymakers work together to eliminate traffic jams and reduce the stress of daily commutes? The answer is yes. Software-defined vehicles, many equipped with advanced traffic management and route optimization systems and already available, can help alleviate congestion. These technologies, combined with emerging business models like shared mobility, multimodal transportation and subscription services may not aim for 'zero' congestion. However, they do offer a way to better manage resources and match demand with supply.

Moreover, new advancements in autonomous driving and connected vehicle technologies, powered by big data, machine learning and AI, are laying the groundwork for a future with minimal traffic congestion. A smoother commute may soon be within reach.

Add to this the principles of the circular economy—design-to-dismantle models, recycling, repurposing end-of-life materials and carbon-neutral logistics—and it's clear that the automotive ecosystem is undergoing a massive, zero-driven transformation

Table 4.1 highlights the zeros that can be applied to the automotive industry.

Table 4.1: Zero in Automotive		
Zero-emissions vehicles	Zero-friction lubrication	Zero-maintenance batteries
Zero-energy vehicles	Zero-glare headlights	Zero-weight tyres
Zero accidents	Zero-fuel vehicles	Zero-idle vehicles
Zero fatalities	Zero-gravity repairs	Zero-friction charging infrastructure
Zero-maintenance vehicles	Zero-gravity tyres	Zero-latency vehicle communication
Zero-gravity automotive	Zero-plastic interiors	Zero-touch autonomous driving
Zero-noise vehicles	Zero-drag aerodynamics	Zero-fatality autonomous vehicle systems
Zero-weight car parts	Zero-touch vehicle interfaces	Zero-collision intersection design
Zero-gap seating	Zero-loss energy transmission	Zero-corrosion vehicle materials
Zero-gravity suspension	Zero-pollution roadways	Zero-weight driver interfaces
Zero-effort steering	Zero-collision traffic systems	Zero congestion
		Zero driving stress

Innovating to Zero in the Commercial Vehicle Industry

When discussing the automotive industry, the focus is often on passenger cars. However, of the approximately 90 million vehicles sold annually, around 15 million are commercial vehicles, including light, medium and heavy trucks, as well as buses.

CHART 4.2 : INNOVATING TO ZERO IN COMMERCIAL VEHICLE INDUSTRY

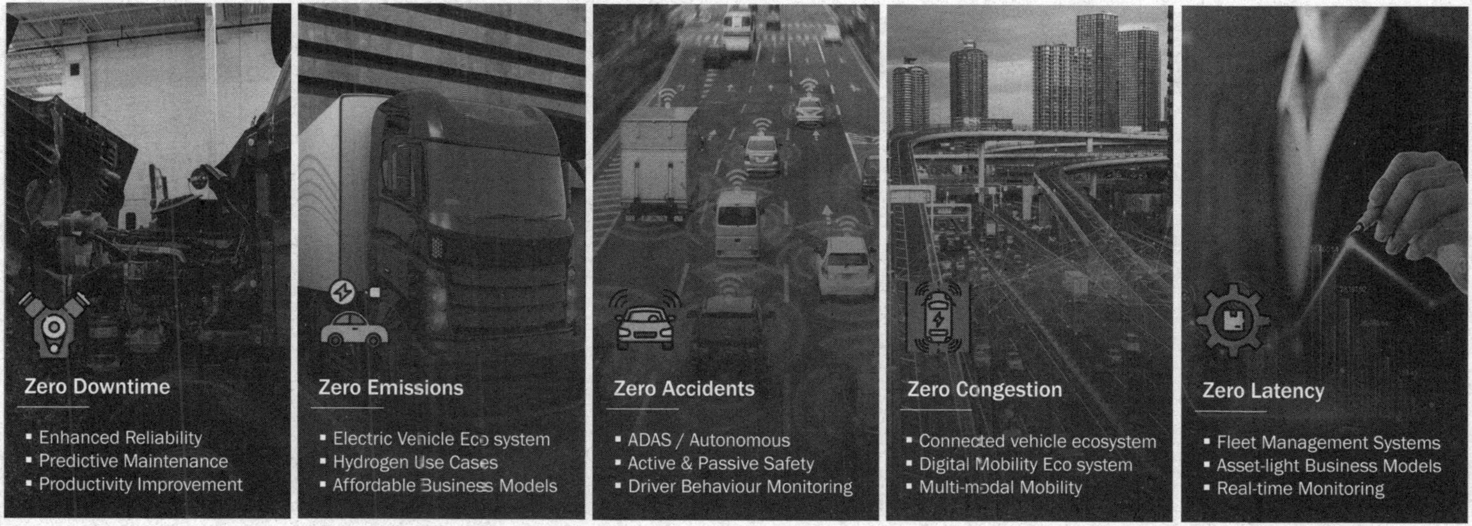

Source : Markets and Markets

Since commercial vehicles cover 50,000 to 80,000 kilometres per year—compared to an average of 15,000 kilometres for passenger cars—their impact on congestion, accidents and, most critically, emissions is significant.

Beyond these 'three evils', the commercial vehicle and logistics sector faces additional challenges. As illustrated in Chart 4.2, this industry, with its narrow profit margins of 2 to 4 per cent and a focus on total cost of ownership (TCO), must also prioritize achieving zero downtime and zero latency. This means minimizing vehicle downtime and optimizing fleet operations through real-time monitoring of vehicles, drivers and goods. Chart 4.2 from MarketsandMarkets highlights the five key 'Zeros' that are crucial for the commercial vehicle industry.

Conclusion

When my book *New Mega Trends* was published, the world was quite different—Tesla was not the force it is today. Fast forward a decade, and like many, I have traded my gas-powered car for a sleek, eco-friendly EV—and, yes, it's a Tesla. For me and many others, the decision to switch has been driven by convenience and a recognition of the future. Once accustomed to the smooth, silent ride of an EV, few would consider going back to an ICE. More importantly, the transition away from conventional fuels aligns with the growing urgency to address climate change and the need for sustainable living.

Having worked in the automotive industry for over thirty years, I firmly believe this industry can lead the charge in achieving a 'zero, zero, zero' future. This means manufacturing ZEVs powered by zero carbon energy. It extends to achieving zero carbon operations in factories, offices and logistics through the adoption of renewable energy. It also includes creating zero-carbon logistics applications and moving to clean, environment-friendly freight transport. It covers zero-carbon supply chains, ensuring sustainability from production to the end-of-life cycle with reuse and recycling practices. The industry must embrace circularity in design, development and delivery to significantly reduce its carbon footprint to nudge it ever closer to zero.[4]

Beyond environmental goals, the automotive industry has the potential to champion diversity and the broader environmental, social, and governance (ESG) agenda. Inclusivity in product and service development is crucial, and the next generation of vans and buses should cater to all drivers—young, old, men and women alike. For the commercial fleet industry, new vehicle designs and technology can attract a wider pool of drivers, helping address labour shortages. Moreover, the integration of ADAS and wellness features can enhance comfort, safety and convenience for drivers and passengers alike, offering personalized solutions rather than one-size-fits-all approaches.

Ultimately, the automotive industry is at the forefront of driving not just a sustainable future, but a more inclusive and socially responsible one. By embracing these opportunities, it can pave the way for a world that is not only greener but more equitable for all.

5

INNOVATING TO ZERO IN THE ENERGY SECTOR

The staggering potential of 'innovating to zero' got me thinking about how it would fit into the energy sector—an industry that, perhaps much more than others, is begging for paradigm shifts. In essence, how would it play out in the highly carbon-intensive energy sector, entailing as it would sweeping changes across power generation, distribution and consumption? Will we see a smooth transition from carbon-intensive, fossil fuels to zero emission, renewable sources? How will zero factor into achieving efficient energy storage and grid technologies? Will it take the form of integrating renewable energy into the grid and supporting reliable, zero-emission power supply? What about smart energy management systems that can enable streamlined, highly efficient, demand-responsive energy distribution, thereby rationalizing energy consumption, while lowering energy losses and emissions? How about clean energy technologies like nuclear or carbon capture and storage (CCS) technologies?

That's a lot to mull over. So if you asked me to summarize the future of energy in one simple sentence, I would say: 'The future of energy will be decarbonized, decentralized, digital and, democratized.'

Decarbonization refers to the shift from fossil fuels to renewable energy sources.

That train has already left the station. The IEA estimates that the share of fossil fuels in electricity generation without carbon capture and utilization (CCU) will fall from 67 per cent in 2020 to about 25 per cent by 2030, before further dropping to almost negligible levels by 2040. Chart 5.1 shows the decline of fossil fuels across power generation, heat generation (buildings and industrial) and road transport. So, zero carbon is already in play in these sectors.

Decentralized refers to the growth of smaller, onsite renewable power generation.

In other words, generation and consumption onsite. A simple example is the installation of solar panels on household rooftops, followed by the consumption of the generated solar energy either by charging batteries to power, say, light bulbs at night or releasing any extra power into the grid.

A decentralized energy solution allows optimal use of renewable power and improves efficiency since it avoids losses associated with moving electricity in the grid from point A to B. A decentralized energy system is a relatively new approach for the energy industry which has traditionally focused on developing mega, centralized power stations and then transmitting the power across long transmission and distribution lines to end users. This brings us to what I would term 'zero-power stations'. Australia has already called a halt to building any new mega fossil fuel power plants. Given the size and spread of the country, it makes perfect sense. Countries like Brazil and China have mega power transmission lines that run over 2,000 km to deliver electricity.

CHART 5.1 : DECARBONIZATION ROADMAP TO 2050

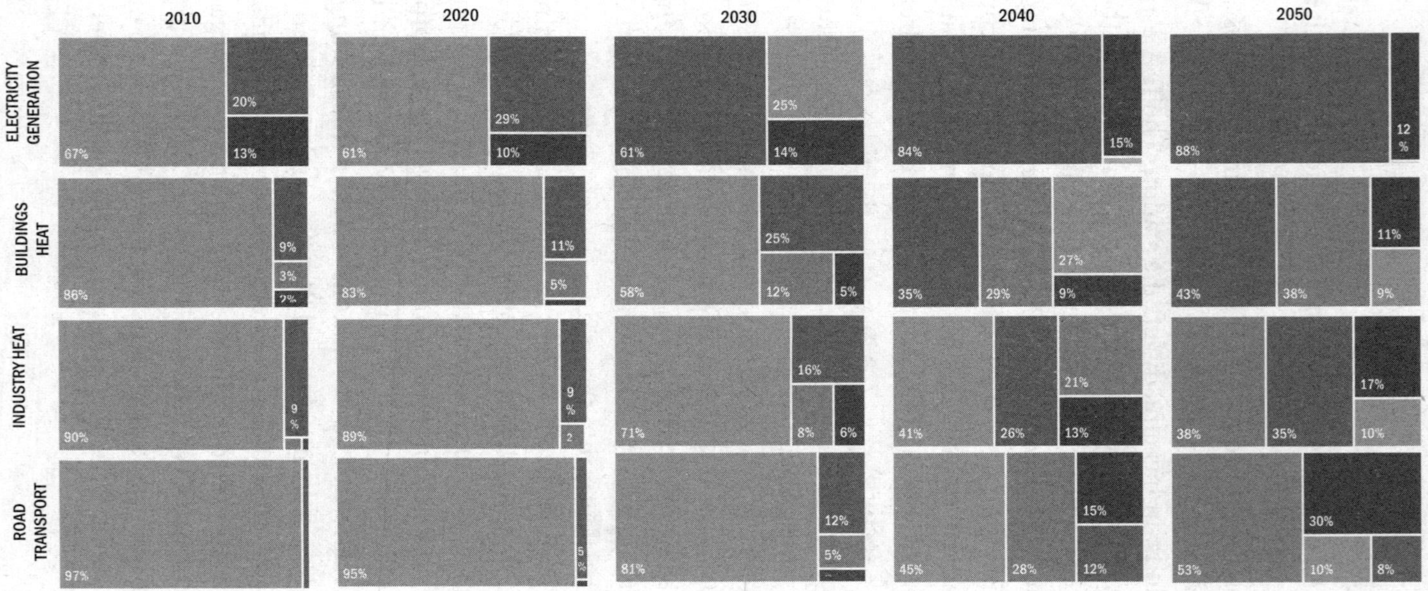

Source : IEA

Imagine the colossal investment and spend on management and maintenance, not to mention environmental impact. With zero-power stations, that investment can be utilized to power individual homes and factories and can give rise to zero transmission and distribution losses. I expect nations to embrace zero-power stations in the future and completely reimagine their transmission and distribution networks.

The third 'D' that will characterize the future of energy is digitalization. In my previous book, I termed this 'smart is the new green', the premise being that green products do not necessarily have a great ROI but if you match them with smart products, then ROI can improve significantly.

'Smart' or 'digital' is all about improving efficiency; it is about convenience, and it is about saving money. Examples of smart and digital products include smart metres, smart buildings, smart charging, smart grids, intelligent grid platforms, and many more. I see huge growth in the digitization of energy infrastructure as it will allow the essential integration of diverse power-generation sources and new technologies. We need energy infrastructure to be monitored in real time, manage and process billions of data points, and automate decision-making. This is where the digitalization of energy becomes critical. A key benefit of digital and smart grids is the instantaneous correction of faults and improved reliability. In a traditional grid, the fault comes to light when the consumer reports it. With a digital grid that uses sensors and communications technology, the fault can be located immediately and potentially resolved remotely. With an AI-enabled grid, the fault can even be predicted based on the certainty that loads will increase due to, say, a storm.

I see numerous opportunities for energy companies in this space, with E.ON One serving as a prime example of innovation.

I recently had the chance to speak with Tim van Amstel, CEO of E.ON One, and hosted a podcast discussing this very topic.

E.ON, a prominent German energy company, operates primarily in grid management and retail, which includes eMobility, energy-infrastructure solutions and energy-supply services. E.ON One, the company's third pillar, is essentially a software company, as Tim describes, aimed at providing fully digital software solutions that support the energy transition.

In simpler terms, Tim defines digital in the energy sector as the ability to create new, interconnected energy-system architectures. The key benefits, according to him, include grid digitization, home energy-management systems (HEMS), eMobility, flexibility (real-time management of demand and supply), efficient heating-grid management and energy monitoring across multiple sites and countries.

With energy demand growing and ever-increasing proportion of renewable energy being fed into the grid, the role of digital tools is becoming critically important in improving the efficiency and efficacy of the modern grid.

The fourth 'D', which is sometimes ignored or underestimated, is democratization of energy. Democratization here refers to making energy accessible to everyone and is based on the localization of solutions. For example, Saudi Arabia has an abundance of sun and fossil fuels, so the country is ripe for developing green-hydrogen solutions. Likewise, Northern England and Northern Europe have an abundance of wind, so the regions can lead with both onshore and offshore wind farms. This is where I believe zero autocracy needs to play a role, which means abandoning energy solutions that fail to harness natural resources in the area to meet the needs of the local population. In other words, does it make sense to put up solar panels in Scotland? Well, not really. But then again, can we innovate and develop cheaper wind farms that can power smaller as well as larger communities in Scotland, and back them with energy-storage solutions? The answer, very simply, is yes, we can, and, yes, we should.

Innovating to zero has a huge role to play in the energy transition. A recent McKinsey report found that reaching net zero by 2050 could entail a 60 per cent increase in capital spending on physical assets, compared with current levels. The report highlighted that investments would be around $9.2 trillion per year until 2050, of which about 70 per cent or roughly $6.5 trillion, would go into low emissions assets and enabling infrastructure, annually. On the flip side, McKinsey analysis shows that growing demand for net-zero offerings could generate more than $12 trillion in annual sales by 2030 across eleven value pools, including transport ($2.3 trillion to $2.7 trillion per year), power ($1.0 trillion to $1.5 trillion) and hydrogen ($650 billion to $850 billion).[1] This huge transformation of the energy sector will create significant growth for climate technologies, solutions and services.

Zero Cost of Energy

Now let us imagine a world where the democratization of energy leads to energy becoming free. Far from being an unbelievable joke, I believe this could be a possible scenario thirty to forty years from today if we keep faith with renewables, solar and cheaper battery solutions. Now imagine what that could mean to future energy solutions like green hydrogen which, today, is expensive to produce at roughly $17–$22 per kg depending upon the market. Currently, blue hydrogen costs roughly about US$2.50–$4 to produce and about the same to convert, store, transport and reconvert for final end use, making it unattractive at between $7–$8.5 per kg. However, imagine that in the future, it becomes free to produce because of an abundance of solar or renewables, with Middle Eastern countries like Saudi Arabia, Qatar, Oman, UAE, and others channeling their widespread availability of fossil fuels and sun to develop green and blue hydrogen. Effectively, one could argue that Middle East could lead, just like they have with fossil fuels, in the production and export of hydrogen. Or, even better, in the development of derivatives of hydrogen like ammonia sulphate, ammonia nitrate, sorbitol, methanol and many others.

Peak Oil and Zero Oil

Every time I have talked about the zero cost of energy, I have evoked strong emotions, particularly among organizations in the oil and gas sector. As the chart created by my team in MarketsandMarkets shows, there are huge differences in perspective when it comes to Peak Oil.

IEA has built three different scenarios as shown in the chart—slightly aggressive, I would say—suggesting that around 2030, we will see Peak Oil. Furthermore, as shown in Chart 5.2, IEC's net-zero scenario suggests oil use will plummet by 2050 from its pre-Covid peak of 100 million barrels per day to about 24 million barrels per day. On the other end of the spectrum, OPEC suggests that oil is here to stay, usage will actually grow to 120 million/barrels, and we will not see a peak before 2050. OPEC's view is that while the oil going into your car's fuel tank might decrease, its use in industry, chemicals and new materials like graphene-based materials will grow.

I believe that the growth in renewables and EVs—where EVs could rise from current rates of just under 15 per cent to comprise 30 per cent of all new vehicle sales by 2030—the decline of oil is clear. As per MarketsandMarkets, peak ICE, as shown in Chart

CHART 5.2 : PEAK OIL

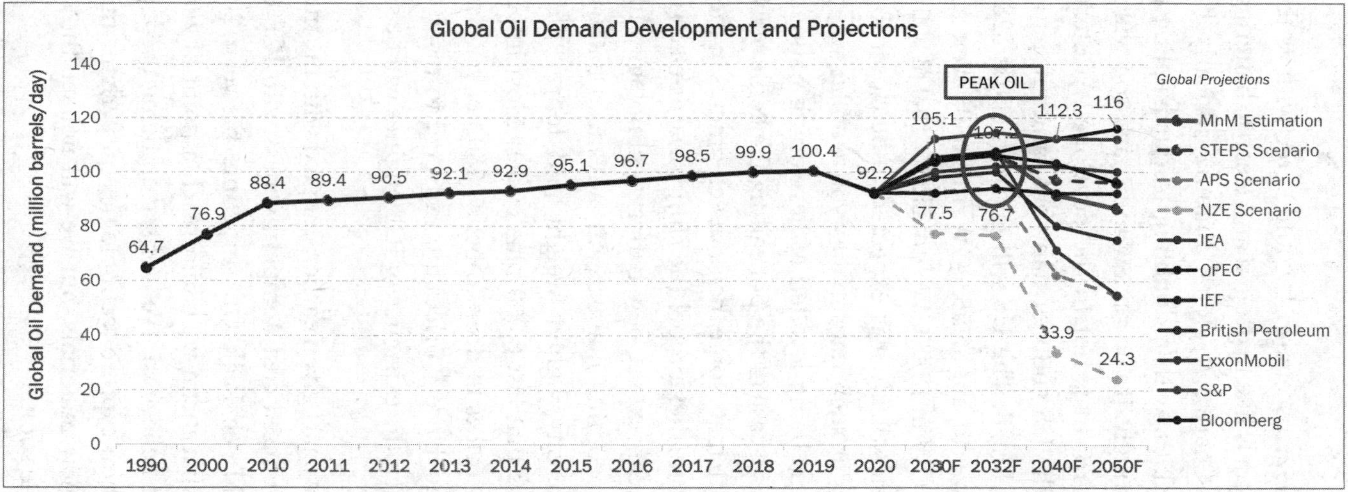

STEPS - Stated Policies Scenario provides a more conservative benchmark for the future, because it does not take it for granted that governments will reach all announced goals.
APS - The Announced Pledges Scenario introduced in 2021 aims to show to what extent the announced ambitions and targets, including the most recent ones, are on the path to deliver emissions reductions required to achieve net zero emissions by 2050
NZE - The Net Zero Emissions by 2050 Scenario (NZE) is a normative IEA scenario that shows a pathway for the global energy sector to achieve net zero CO2 emissions by 2050, with advanced economies reaching net zero emissions in advance of others delivering

Source : Markets and Markets, BP. IEA, S&P, Bloomberg, OPEC and various others

5.2, is likely in 2032, a scenario I would agree with as the world shifts to net-zero fuels like hydrogen and electric batteries.

As shown in Chart 5.3, global roadmaps clearly highlight growth in renewables, with a doubling to quadrupling in most countries. Interestingly, if you review the chart, you will see that this exceptional growth is not in the developed Western world and nations like the US and Germany but rather in nations like China, India and Brazil. The US will go from about 328 GW of renewables in 2021 to about 557 GW in 2030, even as China surges from 1034 GW to 1883 GW. India has a goal of 500 GW for 2030, although realistically it is expected to be closer to around 418 GW. Looking at such data makes you wonder whether the current accusations being levelled at developing nations by the developed world is a case of the pot calling the kettle black.

By 2030, we anticipate some major developments in the battery industry that will further propel the shift towards electrification of transport. We can expect new battery technologies like solid oxide fuel cells becoming mainstream, advanced batteries with higher energy density, lighter weight and longer life cycles, including batteries that last 6,000 plus cycles. Most importantly, we expect battery prices to drop to below $80 per kw. Sometime in the next decade, battery prices are expected to reach $60 per kw and that is when the existence of ICE engines will be seriously questioned.

The data in the chart given earlier, coupled with the increasing affordability of EVs and cost-competitiveness with ICE engines, suggests we could see Peak Oil sometime between 2032 and 2035. Now does that mean we could reach a point of zero oil in the future. I don't believe so. We will see oil being used, perhaps coupled with carbon capture technologies or, perhaps more, like I mentioned, in new materials, but we will not see the death of black gold anytime soon.

CHART 5.3 : RENEWABLE ENERGY DEPLOYMENT BY 2030

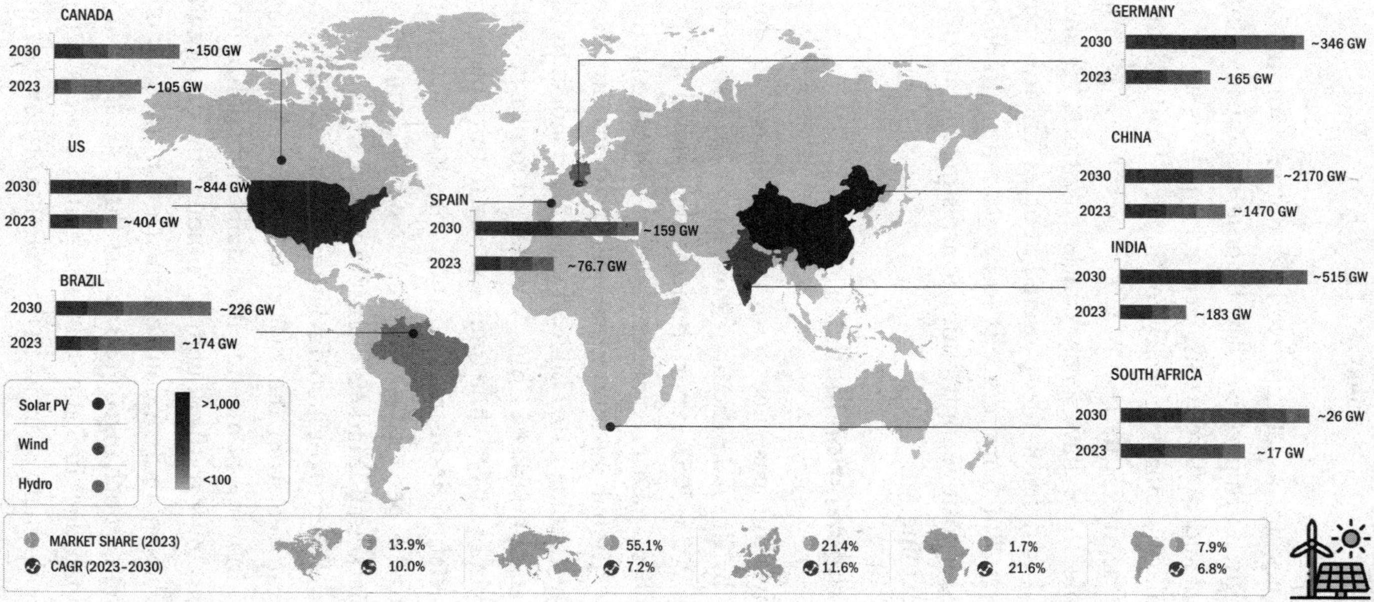

Source: IRENA, IEA, and MarketsandMarkets Analysis

The quest for a net-zero world is not just admirable but is, increasingly, an imperative. It will come accompanied by major challenges and require us to overhaul our lives as we know it. Meanwhile, the energy industry continues to be in the dock as the source of nearly 75 per cent of global greenhouse gas emissions. And while there have been concerted efforts to shift away from coal and fossil fuel-powered sources towards renewable alternatives, much more needs to be done if the industry is to truly make a positive contribution to arresting climate change and global warming.

Zero in the Aviation Industry

Global aviation passenger growth is expected to double by 2045 led by the Asia Pacific region. The World Airport Traffic Forecasts 2023–2052 report projects that global air passenger traffic will surpass pre-pandemic levels and surpass 10 billion in 2025.[2] Global aviation passenger volumes are forecast to eventually double to 19.3 billion by 2042. As shown in Chart 5.4 by MarketsandMarkets, China is expected to overtake the US at the top spot by 2042, while India will rise to third place.

The aviation industry is carbon-intensive and contributes around to 2.5 per cent of the world's carbon emissions. Chart 5.5 by MarketsandMarkets' aerospace team shows the different scenarios related to the global aviation industry's carbon footprint. As you can see from the two charts, the industry has a stiff challenge in terms of meeting its sustainability obligations in the face of passenger traffic doubling. Although the energy efficiency of flying has more than doubled, the carbon intensity of jet fuel has remained unchanged for the last three decades; we are still using standard jet fuel and it has not gotten any cleaner. Biofuels and other alternatives are just a tiny fraction of global demand and

CHART 5.4: GLOBAL AVIATION PASSENGER GROWTH *

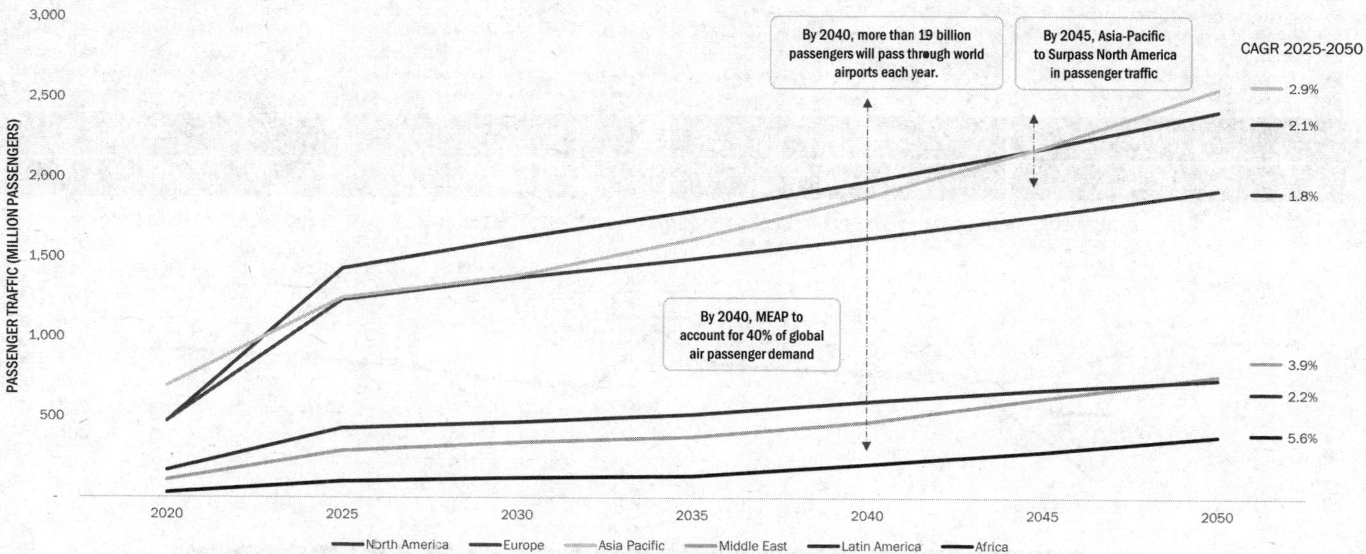

Note: Percentage at the end of each line denotes the CAGP. from 2025-2050

Source: ICAO, IATA, AAI, ITA, CAAC, UN Research Publications, World Bank, MarketsandMarkets Analysis

** From 2023 numbers*

CHART 5.5: CARBON FOOTPRINT SCENARIOS OF AVIATION INDUSTRY TO 2040

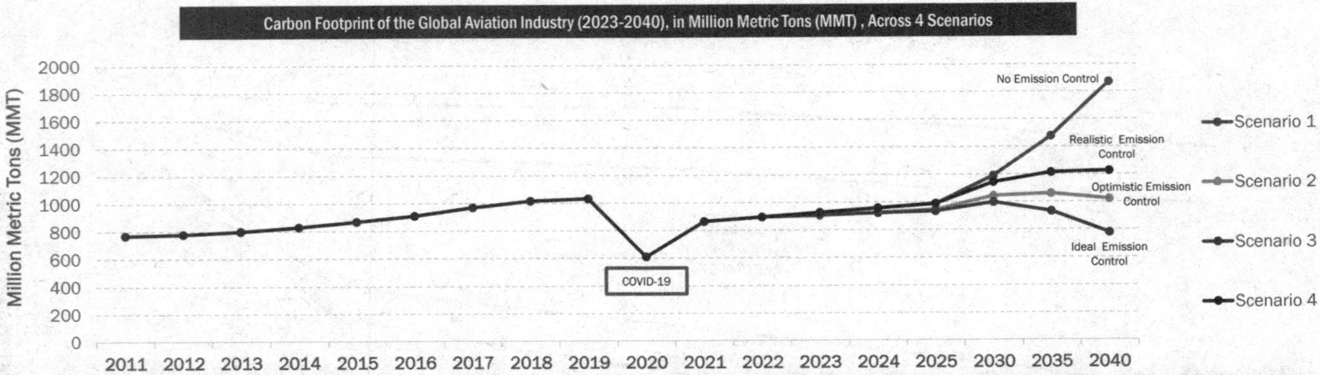

SCENARIO 1	SCENARIO 2	SCENARIO 3	SCENARIO 4
No Emission Control	Optimistic Emission Control	Ideal Emission Control	Realistic Emission Control
▪ 2040 global emission from commercial aviation is projected to be 1,869.1 MMT, in this scenario ▪ This is the highest value among the scenarios and is based on factoring minimal emissions control technologies & incremental flight traffic anticipated	• 2040 global emission from commercial aviation is projected at 1,019.9 MMT, in this scenario • This scenario is optimistic, with wide adoption of SAF, frequent fleet renewals and adoption of hydrogen & electric aircraft platforms in commercial scope	▪ 2040 global emission from commercial aviation is projected at 778.3 MMT, in this scenario ▪ This is the lowest value among the scenarios and lower than pre-COVID levels, driven by standardization of SAF adoption, widespread deployment of hydrogen & electrified platforms	▪ 2040 global emission from commercial aviation is projected at 1223.7 MMT, in this scenario ▪ This scenario factors in realistic levels of adoption of SAF and late emergence and maturation of emission control technologies

Source: MnM Analysis

from my discussions at the recent Farnborough air show in July 2024 in the UK, it does not seem that hydrogen will be viable for long-distance travel before 2040–2045, while electrification will remain limited to small airplanes for short flights as the power to weight ratio of the batteries along with the cost just does not stack up.

A Best-Practice Case Study

Jet Zero Council: A Green Future for Aviation

So, in this fast-paced world of aviation, how do you meet your sustainability goals? Here is where the Jet Zero Council (JZC) is setting its sights on something even more ambitious than just getting people from point A to point B. This unique partnership, which brings together industry, academia and government, is tackling one of the biggest challenges of our time: reducing aviation's carbon footprint. With the goal of achieving at least 10 per cent sustainable aviation fuel (SAF) in the UK's fuel mix by 2030 and zero-emission transatlantic flights within a generation, the JZC is leading the charge towards a more sustainable future in the skies.[3]

By focusing on developing and industrializing zero-emission technologies and establishing UK production facilities for sustainable aviation fuels, the JZC is working to make sure that the future of flying is eco-friendly. This means reducing production costs, driving innovation, and creating a policy and regulatory framework that supports net-zero aviation by 2050. In short, the JZC is putting the pedal to the metal—or perhaps more aptly, the turbine to the wind—in its quest to make green aviation the new normal.

So how exactly does the JZC plan to pull this off? For a start, top-level government and industry leaders are actively collaborating in steering the UK towards net-zero aviation. The council is all about overcoming barriers, whether they be technological, economic or regulatory, to ensure that the UK not only meets but exceeds its climate goals. By accelerating the design, manufacture, testing and certification of zero-emission aircraft and aviation systems, the JZC is working to position the UK as a global leader in green aviation technology.

Recognizing that innovation often starts at the grassroots level, the council has committed to supporting start-ups and disruptors, fostering greater collaboration across sectors, and creating a dynamic ecosystem where new ideas can contribute to the broader goal of zero-emission flight.

A slew of industry heavyweights—Heathrow Airport, easyJet, Rolls-Royce, Manchester Airports Group, Airbus, Boeing, British Airways, and even the Royal Air Force, among others—have signed onto this green revolution. These industry members are leading by example, driving the agenda through tangible actions.

Take Heathrow Airport, for instance. The airport has set ambitious goals for itself, aiming to reduce in-air emissions by up to 15 per cent by 2030, compared to 2019 levels, and ground emissions by at least 45 per cent compared to 2015. Heathrow has also made it clear that 2019 will stand as its peak carbon year, meaning that despite future growth, emissions won't exceed those levels. Heathrow is also using its landing charges to incentivize airlines to increase their use of SAF, working on innovative projects like zero-emission aircraft infrastructure, and even offering a year's free landing to the first commercial zero-emission service to operate from its runways.

Heathrow's efforts also extend to the passengers and staff who pass through its doors. The airport aims for 45 per cent of passengers to use public transport by 2026 and to significantly reduce the number of staff driving to work alone. All airport vehicles are set to be zero-emission by 2030, and Heathrow is even leading the charge in testing low-carbon concrete in its construction projects—a move that could set new standards across the UK.

Preparing UK Airports for Zero-Emission Aircraft

The Zero Emission Flight Infrastructure (ZEFI) programme, spearheaded by the Connected Places Catapult and funded by the Department for Transport, is central to the UK government's plan to achieve net-zero emissions by 2050. As part of the broader Ten Point Plan for a Green Industrial Revolution, ZEFI focuses on preparing the nation's aviation industry for a zero-emission future.

The New Aviation Propulsion Knowledge and Innovation Network (NAPKIN), a consortium which includes Heathrow Airport, Rolls Royce and GKN, has forecast that the UK's entire regional aircraft fleet could be replaced with zero-emission planes by 2040. Hydrogen-fuelled flights could begin as early as 2024, but this shift hinges on developing the necessary infrastructure at UK airports to support these new technologies.

Accordingly, the UK government is actively investing in critical airport infrastructure upgrades to accommodate battery and hydrogen-powered aircraft. However, the success of zero-emission aviation depends on more than just infrastructure—it requires clean fuel production and new regulatory frameworks.

FlyZero, a project led by the Aerospace Technology Institute and supported by the government, is exploring the technical, economic, infrastructural and operational aspects of hydrogen-powered flights, charting a path to make sustainable aviation a reality.

The Jet Zero Council represents a full-throttle effort to transform aviation as we know it. Through sustained investment in research and development, the establishment of SAF production facilities, and the acceleration of zero-emission technologies, the JZC is proving that a greener future for aviation isn't just possible, it's within reach.

In addition to these challenges, we are seeing some interesting trends like hypersonic travel. It is possible that in the distant future, we will be able to fly from New York to London in ninety minutes, thanks to companies like Destinus. This Swiss start-up aims to 'test a supersonic hydrogen prototype' which it claims will be 'the first in the history of aviation' by 2026 and build a hypersonic airplane by 2030.[4] Interestingly, Destinus plans to use liquid hydrogen for its hypersonic aircraft as it bids to achieve its motto Reaching the Future Faster.

Zero in Airports

Typically airport operations can be broken into three parts:

- Landside, which relates to everything from the car parks, to check in counters and immigration. It is typically accessible by the members of the public.
- Airside, which relates to everything on the runway from the planes to the ground transport that helps passengers and

Chart 5.6: Zero in Airports

Source: *MarketsandMarkets Analysis*

freight embark and disembark. This area is restricted for general public.

- Operations, which relates to managing the airport. Typical airport operators like Heathrow are mega project-management companies as they manage over 80,000 employees, and only about 10 per cent of these are their own staff. Heathrow is the single largest site employer in the UK by a long mile.

Chart 5.6 shows examples of how Zero can be applied to airports of the future, from zero baggage delays to net zero airports. Key here is how zero can be applied to improve passenger experience as at the end of the day, the airport operators' motto is to provide you a unique experience and, at the same time, boost their non-aeronautical revenues through having passengers go through zero queues in immigration or security.

6

INNOVATING TO ZERO IN THE CHEMICALS SECTOR

The main drive to zero in the chemical industry currently revolves around zero carbon emissions. This is a major challenge for an industry that is highly energy-intensive, particularly sectors like cement, steel and glass production that require high temperatures and substantial energy consumption. These sectors are now intensely focused on reducing their carbon emissions to zero. Key strategies have been brought into play to reach the industry's net-zero target by 2050: operational decarbonization, carbon capture and storage (CCS) technologies, and renewable and sustainable feedstocks. The electrification of plants and incorporating green hydrogen directly into industrial processes, such as using it in blast furnaces or relying on biomass as a carbon source to reduce metal-ore usage, are just some of the approaches being adopted. Beyond that, the broader chemical industry is working on producing zero carbon products, ranging from resins and polymers to coatings.

A disruptive innovation that aligns with this zero-emissions ambition is the push to use zero crude-oil feedstock. In this regard, hydrogen steps up as a game changer, not only for its potential in clean energy but also in producing eFuels and eChemicals.

As the name suggests, rather than being manufactured through traditional refining, eFuels are electrically produced and are touted to be the fuels of the future. These liquid fuels are not linked to batteries but can serve as direct drop-in replacements for gasoline and diesel. While they are chemically very similar to their fossil-fuel counterparts, eFuels are dissimilar in that they are derived from water and carbon dioxide (or biomass) using electricity. They have the added benefit of being much lower in sulphur and other contaminants, making them cleaner alternatives.

eFuels are created by splitting water into hydrogen and oxygen using electrolysis—an energy-intensive process that, when powered by renewable sources like solar or wind power, is incredibly clean. The green hydrogen produced is then combined with captured carbon dioxide or carbon monoxide in a Fischer-Tropsch reaction to create e-gasoline, e-diesel, e-jet fuel and other e-heating fuels. What makes this even more environment friendly is that the carbon dioxide used can either be captured from industrial emissions or pulled directly from the atmosphere, further reducing the overall carbon footprint.

There are other emerging technologies for producing e-Fuels, such as direct electrolysis of carbon dioxide, microbial electrosynthesis, photoelectric synthesis and plasma-based conversion. But the Fischer-Tropsch process is by far the most industrialized and widely adopted.

Another innovation on the road to zero crude-oil dependency is biorefining, which merges the concepts of zero carbon and zero oil feedstocks. Biorefining involves producing chemicals in bioreactors through processes like fermentation or pyrolysis. Chemicals such as succinic acid, lactic acid, glycols, ethylene, ethanol and methane can be derived from biomass, with the ultimate goal being the use of household waste as feedstock.

While there has been considerable interest and investment in biorefining, and companies like BioAmber have successfully produced bio-based chemicals as drop-in replacements for crude oil chemicals such as succinic acid, the sector has faced challenges. Competing with the cost-efficiency of oil-based alternatives is difficult, particularly when oil prices drop, often undermining these nascent ventures. However, with the rising focus on zero carbon and sustainability, companies involved in biorefining are gaining new momentum.

Zero Accidents and Zero Plant Downtime

Moving beyond emissions, achieving zero accidents and zero plant downtime remains a top priority for the chemical industry. This has always been a fundamental goal, especially given the catastrophic consequences of industrial failures such as the Bhopal gas tragedy in India in 1984, where a pesticide plant leak resulted in thousands of deaths. But more recently too, plant accidents and shutdowns have plagued the chemical supply chain, reminding us of the need for constant vigilance. A fire at BASF's Ludwigshafen plant in 2017 caused a shutdown and force majeure on some of its products, affecting many downstream markets. Another fire—this time at Huntsman's MDI site in August 2024—was similarly attributed to force majeure. Digital monitoring, sensors and predictive maintenance, powered by AI and other advanced tools, are becoming essential to prevent accidents and minimize downtime. These technologies offer real-time insight into plant conditions, enabling early detection of potential problems and making the goal of zero accidents and zero downtime more attainable.

Zero Reliance on Overseas Suppliers

Another key objective for many companies in the chemicals industry is zero reliance on specific geopolitical regions, particularly China. The COVID-19 pandemic underscored the vulnerability of global supply chains, bringing into particularly sharp focus how dependent many businesses had become on Chinese supply chains. As a result, companies are now looking to reshore some of their operations, or at least diversify their supplier base, to reduce risks. Technologies like 3D printing and industrial automation are playing a big role here. With 3D printing and industrial automation, companies require less labour (which translates to lower associated costs) and can produce plastic and metal parts locally. This technology allows for greater flexibility, faster production, and ultimately, reduced dependence on low-cost overseas suppliers.

Beyond Zero Carbon

While zero carbon is the immediate goal, it's only part of the picture. The next frontier could involve tackling other harmful emissions. Zero NOx and SOx emissions—nitrogen and sulphur oxides that contribute to air pollution—are becoming key targets, especially as governments clamp down on vehicle exhaust fumes.

Then there's the issue of zero heavy metals. Heavy metals like mercury and chromium can bioaccumulate, especially in marine ecosystems, leading to contamination of fish stocks. In the digital and electrical age, where metals are more heavily used in technologies like electric vehicle motors and batteries, managing heavy metal disposal and manufacturing waste will become increasingly important. The industry is already addressing chromium removal in cement production, but we're likely to see more focus on heavy metals in the years to come. Accordingly, disposal and manufacturing waste will need to be addressed and monitored.

Zero Water Pollution

Zero water pollution is also climbing the agenda, particularly as the demand for clean, fresh water intensifies. Technologies like Zero Water Discharge (ZWD) systems, which can treat and reuse wastewater on-site, are becoming more appealing. Although current regulations don't require widespread adoption of these systems, public pressure is growing. We're seeing increased awareness of the state of our rivers and lakes, driven by high-profile events like the 2024 Paris Olympics, where the poor water quality of the River Seine had to be addressed before triathletes were ready to take the plunge.

This rising concern is likely to spur governments and water companies into action, and we can expect a push for technologies that address water pollution, such as active pollutant removal systems for chemicals like PFAS from ground and water sources. With these developments, opportunities for ZWD systems, water centrifuges and spiral membranes are set to grow.

Conclusion

The chemicals industry is on an ambitious path to zero with zero carbon emissions, zero accidents, zero crude-oil reliance, zero plant downtime, and zero environmental impact. From eFuels and biorefining to advanced digital monitoring and sustainable supply chains, from tackling other harmful emissions to working on eliminating water pollution, the pursuit of a sustainable chemical industry is well underway.

7

INNOVATING TO ZERO IN THE HEALTHCARE SECTOR

Defining and Achieving Zero Goals for Patient Outcomes and Care Delivery Operations

In *New Mega Trends*, I had predicted that while sustainability and the environment would be the biggest mega trends of the decade, the next decade would belong to healthcare. Sure enough, rampant climate change and extreme weather events have made sustainability and decarbonization an ongoing imperative. And then, almost on cue, our lives were turned upside down in the early 2020s with the pandemic. It bore out my prediction that this decade would belong to the mega trend of health, wellness and wellbeing. Were we to follow the logic of the Kondratieff Cycles, healthcare could represent the next major cycle, stretching to 2050 and beyond.

Globally, the flow of money supports the critical importance of this trend. Healthcare spending in the Western world is already, on average, between 12 per cent and 18 per cent of GDP. To put things in perspective, the US spent over $4.8 trillion on healthcare in 2023[1], marking a 7.5 per cent increase over 2022, and outpacing GDP growth of 6.1 per cent. This rate of growth puts developed economies on track to spend almost 20 per cent of their GDP on healthcare by 2032. Even for the largest economy of the world, this is a very high value, given that OECD members average 13.35 per cent, while the world cumulatively spends about 10.35 per cent of its GDP on healthcare.[2] In almost all countries worldwide, per capita healthcare spending is rising faster than per capita income and, if this trend continues, healthcare spending as a percentage of GDP will more or less double over the next twenty to thirty years. Healthcare spending in the US could surge to almost 30 per cent by 2050. These levels of spending are unsustainable, and something will have to give. This is why President Obama used so much of his political capital during his first few years in office to revamp the healthcare system—he and his team knew that the rates of spending on healthcare had to be modified dramatically to avoid the dire economic consequences resulting from expending 20 to 30 per cent of the country's GDP on healthcare while, at the same time, shouldering a massive debt burden.

A rethink of current healthcare models is inevitable. Countries around the world are being forced to ramp up public expenditure on healthcare, owing to an aging population (10 per cent of the world's population is now sixty-five years old and above,[3] an age group which also suffers from co-morbidities or from diseases like cancer (53 per cent of all cancer patients are above the age of 65)[4] that have costly treatment regimes. In addition, younger populations are increasingly being afflicted with cardiovascular conditions (38 per cent of premature deaths are caused by cardiovascular conditions[5] and diabetes (with its incidence set to grow 46 per cent from 2021 to 2045.[6] Despite the escalating outlays on healthcare, we have not yet managed to check the rise of diseases.

According to WHO, one in six people will be aged sixty years by 2030, with this population cohort on track to expand from 1 billion in 2020 to 1.4 billion by 2030. By 2050, the number of people aged sixty years and older will double to 2.1 billion, and the number of people aged eighty years or older will triple between 2020 and 2050 to reach 426 million.

People aged over sixty years utilize three to five times more healthcare services than younger people. It is estimated that 75 per cent of people aged over sixty years have at least one chronic condition, while over 50 per cent have two or more chronic conditions.[7] It is worth noting here that chronic diseases account for more than 60 per cent of all healthcare spending. In parallel, lifespans are increasing. One in six people in Western economies today will now live to blow out one hundred candles from their birthday cakes, while the person who will live the grand old age of 150 years has already been born. Such demographic data taken in consonance with data on unsustainable health economics dictate a shift in spending paradigms—away from treatment and towards predicting, diagnosing and monitoring.

Accordingly, we have seen a change in healthcare business models over the last decade with the focus moving away from the conventional approach of treating symptoms towards a more holistic, preventative model of prediction, early diagnosis and ongoing monitoring.

Health wearables have become ubiquitous, tracking a broad spectrum of metrics, including sleep patterns, heart rate, oxygen levels, blood pressure, physical fitness and emotional states. These devices are instrumental in preventing chronic conditions such as diabetes and cardiovascular disease by enabling individuals to continually monitor their health.

Sensors integrated into smart watches for blood glucose measurement are poised to make diabetes management more convenient. The next big thing are smart rings—the Oura Ring 3 or the Samsung Galaxy Ring are on my Christmas list—that monitor a range of health parameters from sleep, stress, fitness levels, body temperature, heart rate, oxygen levels and activity levels, among others.

Smart clothes now range from socks to shoes, work attire to casual wear, sleepwear to activewear with functions that cover fitness tracking to body monitoring. So, for instance, Under Armour's Athlete Recovery sleepwear aids with sleep quality and muscle recovery, Ralph Lauren's PoloTech T-shirts track fitness activity and suggest training regimes.

Hearables, wearable devices with headphone functionalities, are enhancing hearing health. Smart bandages with integrated sensors are monitoring moisture levels, temperature and infections in real time to promote targeted treatment and assist with wound healing.

Implantable devices support the functioning of organs like the heart and brain. Future developments may include insideables like smart pills that communicate data, say, glucose levels or transmit internal images that aid in determining the best clinical approach.

Artificial intelligence is revolutionizing healthcare by enabling the early and precise diagnosis of various cancers and mental-health conditions. AI-based symptom-tracking apps and voice and speech recognition software can identify signs of physical, mental and emotional stress, alerting healthcare providers to potential issues in real time. Furthermore, AI-based video games are being developed to enhance the attention spans of young children.

Emerging technologies promise to further transform healthcare outcomes. CRISPR, an advanced gene-editing technology, holds the potential to address major health issues, including cancer, HIV, rare diseases and genetic defects. 3D printing is already employed to create customized implants, prosthetics and replacement joints, with future smart 3D pills likely to aid patients in managing multiple medications. Bioprinting shows promise in regenerating skin cells for burn victims, blood vessels, synthetic ovaries and even a pancreas. Neuralink, a brain-computer interface developed by Elon Musk, aims to convert thoughts into actions, enabling paralysed individuals to control digital devices mentally.

Future of Healthcare

At MarketsandMarkets, we highlight five key themes that define the health industry. See Chart 7.1.

Burden of Disease

Over the past few decades, the global burden of disease has markedly shifted from infectious diseases to chronic and non-communicable diseases (NCDs) such as cardiovascular diseases, cancer, diabetes and chronic respiratory conditions. NCDs are now responsible for approximately 74 per cent of all deaths globally, with 41 million people dying each year from them.[8] This epidemiological transition has profound implications for both mortality and economic stability. Indirect mortality from NCDs is significant, often resulting from complications and comorbidities that exacerbate the severity of other health conditions. Economically, NCDs impose a substantial burden through increased healthcare costs, loss of productivity and long-term disability. For instance, it is estimated that between 2010 and 2030, the top five NCDs will cost the global economy $47 trillion.[9] These diseases necessitate prolonged medical treatment and management which can strain health systems and deplete financial resources at both individual and national levels. Moreover, the

CHART 7.1: FIVE THEMES DEFINING THE HEALTH INDUSTRY

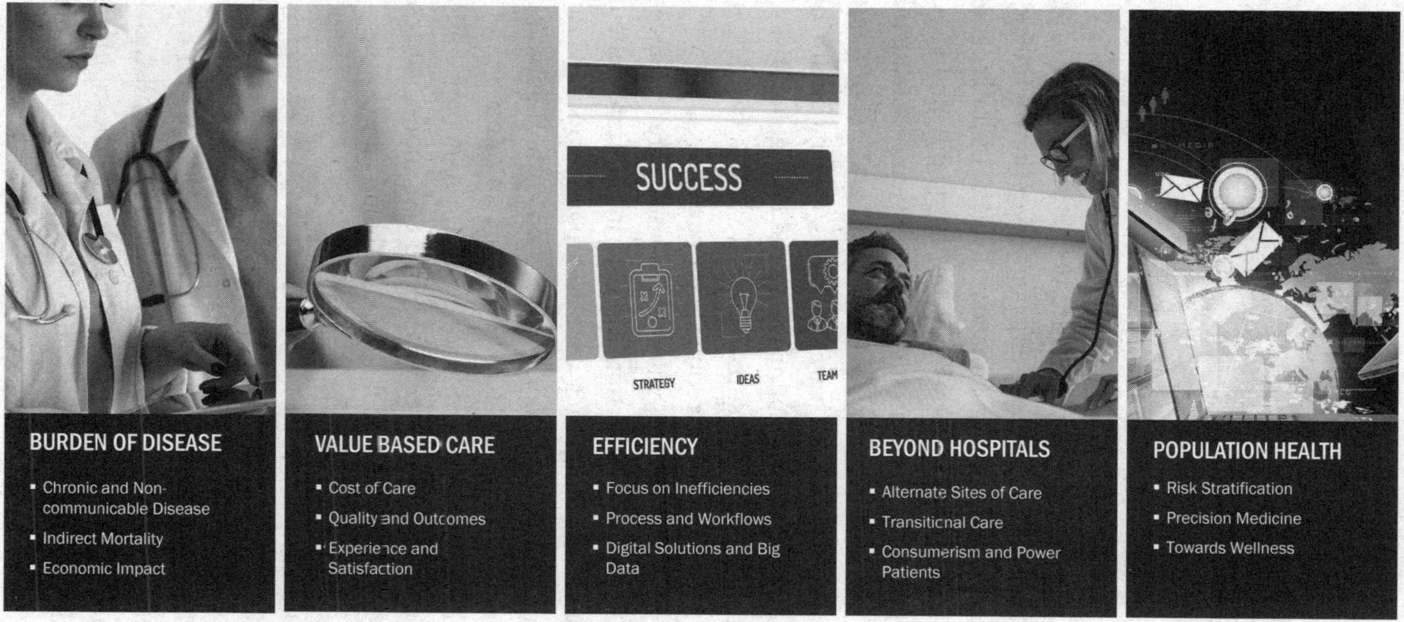

Source : MarketsandMarkets

rising prevalence of NCDs hinders economic growth by reducing workforce productivity and adding to social-welfare costs, thereby creating a cyclical impact on economies worldwide.

Value-Based Care

Value-based care is a healthcare delivery model that prioritizes patient outcomes and cost-efficiency over the volume of services provided. This approach aims to reduce the overall cost of care by incentivizing providers to focus on the quality and effectiveness of treatments rather than the quantity. By emphasizing preventive care, chronic disease management and coordinated care pathways, value-based care improves patient health outcomes and reduces hospital readmissions and emergency visits. Quality and outcomes are measured through various metrics, including patient-recovery rates, reduced complications and overall health improvements. Additionally, value-based care enhances patient experience and satisfaction by fostering a more patient-centric approach, ensuring that care is tailored to individual needs and preferences. This holistic focus on cost, quality and patient experience ultimately leads to a more sustainable and efficient healthcare system, with better health outcomes and higher patient satisfaction. The value-based care model is becoming an important contender to help control healthcare costs.

Efficiency

Healthcare efficiency has become increasingly critical in recent years due to spiraling costs, aging populations, and the growing prevalence of chronic diseases. Soaring demand has not been matched by a proportionate growth in healthcare infrastructure and skilled manpower, thereby underlining the urgent need for greater process and operational efficiencies. The pandemic further exacerbated an already dire situation with clinician burnouts from which healthcare systems are still recovering. Improving operational efficiencies is, therefore, paramount, with a focus on streamlining—or, for that matter, even eliminating—administrative, manual and redundant tasks. Nurses and doctors who spend valuable, productive time, often several hours each day, on energy-sapping administrative paperwork can be helped with digital automation solutions that free them up to focus on their core role and on what really matters—patient care. By leveraging digital tools and insights, healthcare systems can achieve greater efficiency, ultimately improving patient outcomes and reducing overall healthcare costs. Post-pandemic, there has been increasing demand for solutions such as nurse scheduling, operating room block utilization and enterprise-level patient flow that enhance operational efficiency. At the same time, the hope is that clinicians will be able to spend less time on administrative tasks and, therefore, enjoy a better work–life balance and quality of life. Needless to add, this will positively impact performance and productivity.

Beyond Hospitals

The shift of patient care settings from hospitals to external environments, including to home settings, has been a significant trend in recent years. It has been driven by the need to enhance patient convenience, reduce healthcare costs and improve outcomes. Outpatient clinics, home healthcare, telemedicine and ambulatory care services are becoming increasingly popular alternatives to traditional hospital-based care. This transition is being fuelled by advancements in medical technology and digital health, enabling many procedures and treatments to be safely and effectively administered in less intensive settings. By moving care closer to where patients live, these approaches reduce the need for hospital admissions and lower the risk of hospital-acquired infections. Additionally, they offer patients greater comfort and flexibility, often resulting in higher satisfaction and adherence to treatment plans. Health systems benefit from reduced strain on hospital resources, enabling them to focus on more critical and complex cases. This shift also aligns with value-based care models, which prioritize outcomes and cost-efficiency over the volume of services provided, ultimately fostering a more sustainable and patient-centred healthcare system.

Population Health

Population health management is becoming a focal point in healthcare, emphasizing the need to improve health outcomes for entire populations. A key component of this approach is risk stratification, which involves categorizing patients based on their health risks and tailoring interventions accordingly. By identifying high-risk individuals, healthcare providers can proactively manage chronic conditions, prevent disease progression and reduce healthcare costs. Precision medicine complements this by using genetic, environmental and lifestyle data to develop personalized treatment plans that are more effective for individual patients. This approach ensures that interventions are specifically targeted, maximizing their efficacy and chances of success. Additionally, there is a growing emphasis on wellness and preventive care, with a holistic focus on maintaining health and preventing disease, rather than a more limited view of solely treating the disease. This wellness-oriented methodology includes promoting healthy lifestyles, regular screenings and early interventions, which collectively contribute to better health outcomes and lower healthcare expenditures. By integrating risk stratification, precision medicine, and a wellness-focused strategy, population health management aims to create a more proactive, efficient and patient-centred healthcare system.

The future holds intriguing propositions: healthcare that will be truly personalized, driven by genomics as well as by continuous monitoring of a person's vitals. These vitals—beyond the handful that are tracked today (yes, I diligently do my 10,000 steps every day, thank you very much)—will be monitored by wearables, implants or fixed sensors in homes, offices, cars and our surroundings in general. They will also be capable of monitoring a variety of analytes in our body, not just glucose levels. What's more, these solutions will monitor these vitals in real time, immediately diagnose any issues or anomalies and recommend tweaks to treatments.

Democratization of knowledge and know-how, together with wider access to technology, will be the lynchpin in addressing healthcare disparities and ensuring that most people have access to basic health monitoring capabilities. Gene-therapy advancements will likely help treat myriad genetic conditions including, possibly, cancer. Regenerative medicine and tissue engineering will offer new alternatives to organ transplants or for pancreatic cells secreting insulin for diabetics.

Geriatric care has become increasingly important as populations age. Technology will help the elderly to be continuously monitored in the comfort of their homes. Loneliness and social isolation have become major health concerns, particularly among the elderly. Studies reveal that almost half of adults in the US have experienced loneliness on an everyday basis. Research indicates that loneliness has devastating health consequences: it is linked to a 26 per cent increase in the risk of premature death and heightened levels of dementia, depression, stroke and cardiovascular disease.[10] Technology is helping alleviate loneliness with robotic companions and even robotic animal companions.

Tellingly, new paradigms in healthcare will mean that hospitals and healthcare systems, as we know them today, will cease to exist. After all, once most people start receiving monitoring and treatment services with advanced AI support, health complications will be effectively managed outside hospital settings. This will limit hospitals to dealing with only very severe medical cases. Post-surgery recovery will also be pushed out to home environments, thanks to the prospect of continuous monitoring. Moreover, clinics in their current form will no longer exist since video conferencing has already made it possible for consultations to occur online. Portable medical devices, including complex MRI machines, may become available for home diagnosis, allowing nurses to scan patients in their homes.

Overall, people will lead longer, high-quality lifespans.

The Quintuple Aim of Healthcare

In 2007, the Institute for Healthcare Improvement introduced the Triple Aim of Healthcare: improving the patient experience, improving patient outcomes and reducing per capita cost of care. In 2015, another dimension of 'improving the clinician's experience' was added to this framework to form the Quadruple Aim of Healthcare. And after witnessing the aftermath of the COVID-19 pandemic, another long-standing need was added in 2022—that of health equity—forming the Quintuple Aim of Healthcare.

What is incredible to note here is that despite it being seventeen years since its inception, we are nowhere close to achieving any of the goals mentioned in the original Triple Aim, and have actually ended up adding a couple more along the way. Indeed, these goals are not meant to be destinations but rather journeys, the intention behind them being to guide us in transforming our approach to care delivery.

While we are spending more on healthcare to address the rising demand for care, a looming crisis is the shortage of healthcare workers and trained clinicians. By 2030, the healthcare industry anticipates a shortfall of 10 million workers.[11] This is where digital technologies will come to the rescue, making a huge impact in terms of achieving clinical excellence, improving operational efficiency, and boosting overall patient and clinician experiences. The top eight technologies, namely, connectivity (5G, 6G), big data and predictive analytics, cloud and edge computing, virtual and augmented reality, digital twins, drones, AI and IoT sensors for connected living are anticipated to have the greatest impact in the coming decades. These technologies are being tested and piloted globally, with some already having been commercially implemented.

While we move forward towards the future of healthcare, concepts such as personalized medicine and precision health are becoming commonplace. These will be aided by enabling technologies and shaped by the challenges discussed here.

The Zero-X Goals for Healthcare

Beyond healthcare, we face other broader challenges, such as climate change, that motivated the establishment of the United Nations' Sustainable Development Goals (SDGs), many of which also impact the healthcare industry. These may well inspire the development of net-zero goals for the healthcare industry, in line with the Quintuple Aim of Healthcare.

A sample of such net-zero goals:

No.	Goal	Category
1	Zero surgery errors	Clinical excellence
2	Zero invasive surgery	Clinical excellence
3	Zero diseases	Clinical excellence
4	Zero infections	Clinical excellence
5	Zero readmissions	Clinical excellence
6	Zero unplanned reoperations	Clinical excellence
7	Zero preventable deaths	Clinical excellence
8	Zero-waste medication	Clinical excellence
9	Zero harmful medication errors	Clinical excellence
10	Zero falls	Clinical excellence
11	Zero medication non-adherence	Clinical excellence
12	Zero needlestick injuries	Clinical excellence
13	Zero-error pathology	Clinical excellence
14	Zero antibiotic resistance	Clinical excellence
15	Zero paperwork	Clinician experience
16	Zero physician burnouts	Clinician experience
17	Zero-plastic healthcare	Healthcare manufacturing
18	Zero medical-device recalls	Healthcare manufacturing
19	Net zero hospitals	Healthcare operations
20	Zero medical waste	Healthcare operations
21	Zero-deficit health system	Healthcare operations
22	Zero-carbon healthcare facilities	Healthcare operations
23	Zero healthcare fraud	Healthcare operations
24	Zero-emission ambulances	Healthcare operations
25	Zero-delay surgery	Healthcare operations

26	Zero-defect sterilization	Healthcare operations
27	Zero-carbon hospitals	Healthcare operations
28	Zero-error electronic health records	Healthcare operations
29	Zero-waste healthcare	Healthcare operations
30	Zero-wait time healthcare	Patient experience
31	Zero-late appointments	Patient experience
32	Zero patient complaints	Patient experience
33	Zero-ageism	Patient experience
34	Zero hunger*	Social determinants of healthcare
35	Zero malnutrition	Social determinants of healthcare
36	Zero child malnutrition	Social determinants of healthcare
37	Zero tolerance for health disparities	Social determinants of healthcare
38	Zero obesity	Wellness focus
39	Zero-calorie foods	Wellness focus
40	Zero-sugar drinks	Wellness focus
41	Zero-alcohol policy	Wellness focus

*A United Nations Sustainable Development Goal

Effectively, these goals represent a broader movement in the healthcare industry from short-term goals to a more long-term vision, offering glimpses into the future trajectory of healthcare.

1. *Clinical excellence* that directly impacts patient-health outcomes, together with *clinician experience* and *patient experience*, tie in directly with three of the quintuple aims. These are in focus today, especially with the thrust on

alleviating the burden of administrative tasks on doctors with a view to reducing burnouts, an issue that peaked during and after the pandemic.

2. *Healthcare operations* goals are tied to two major themes: firstly, improving operational margins, which took a major hit during the pandemic and started showing signs of recovery only in 2023 and, secondly, helping achieve long-term climate action goals.
3. *Social determinants of healthcare goals*—zero hunger, zero malnutrition and zero child malnutrition—are so-called owing to the larger umbrella under which they fall, that is, health equity. The goal around health disparities is slightly different and is also representative of the fifth and the most recent addition to the quintuple aim, that is, health equity. The aim here is to promote equal access and distribution of health gains, particularly to socially, economically, geographically and demographically marginalized groups. All these goals are poised to make a deep impact in the long run.
4. *Wellness-focused goals* point to the long-term focus on preventive healthcare to ensure healthier lifestyles.

Digital technologies will be key enablers in empowering the healthcare industry to achieve these goals. However, achieving them remains an uphill task, requiring navigating through a complex maze of regulations and policies, economic considerations, patient behavior, healthcare access and more.

Zero Obesity

Obesity is now recognized as a disease, although this was not the case historically when it was seen as a 'failure of character' or the result of weak willpower. It took the WHO to declare obesity a disease for it to be considered as such. However, the widespread acceptance of obesity being a disease was not achieved until the 2010s. For instance, it was only in 2013 that the American Medical Association voted to recognize it as a disease. Today, we are in the midst of an obesity epidemic, with WHO estimating a whopping 2.5 billion adults globally to be overweight, of whom around 890 million are obese.[12] For reference, while 43 per cent of adults were considered overweight in 2022, only 25 per cent were overweight in 1990, indicating a near-doubling of obesity rates.

This silent epidemic shows no signs of abating and is worrisome because of the serious health complications that typically accompany obesity—diabetes, cardiovascular conditions, stroke, high blood pressure, and a host of other health issues. WHO estimates obesity to have led to 5 million deaths premature deaths in 2019 alone, making it one of the leading causes of death linked to NCDs. In contrast, the COVID-19 pandemic has, to date, resulted in a total of 7 million deaths. The World Obesity Federation predicts that by 2030, one in five women and one in seven men will suffer from obesity. By 2030, issues related to obesity and being overweight are projected to cost $3 trillion annually, and top $18 trillion by 2060 if left unchecked.

From multiple standpoints then, zero obesity is a must-achieve objective. From an obese patient's perspective—those who have known for a long time that 'willpower' alone won't help—medications like GLP1 have proven to be highly effective in helping reduce body weight by 15–20 per cent. Originally developed as a treatment for type-2 diabetes, it took some time for researchers to explore the effects on weight loss of these medications. Although the first versions of GLP1s for diabetes have been around since 2005, its use for weight-loss was named as the Science Breakthrough of the Year in 2023.[13]

Medicines apart, another strategy to tackle obesity has been to tax junk food. 'Government cannot legislate morality but can tax sin' is a position that governments in countries like Hungary and Denmark have embraced while introducing the so-called 'fat tax'. Consider your favourite indulgences like burgers, fizzy drinks, chocolates, crisps, sweets and ice creams costing up to 20 per cent more. Governments have realized that by raising taxes on cigarettes, they have managed to discourage consumption, control smoking-related illnesses and, at the same time, generate much-needed tax revenue. This strategy is now being applied to unhealthy foods. Like it or not, eating that quarter pounder with a jumbo chocolate thick shake at your favourite fast-food joint will end up being an extremely expensive proposition in the future, one that will weigh heavily on your wallet and conscience, even as the government builds up its coffers. A bitter pill for junk food companies to swallow but sweet news for consumers and public health authorities. Perhaps time to ditch all things deep-fried, salt-laden and sugar-filled items for all things fresh, organic, and wholesome.

The goal of zero obesity is now clearly within reach and the impact it can have on all of us, whether individually or collectively, and on global healthcare systems is tremendous. Keeping the weight off after discontinuing obesity medication will be a new opportunity area for healthcare systems and the wellness culture. I foresee a positive culture of health and fitness flourishing, spearheaded by the previously obese and overweight, heralding a virtuous cycle of change. Targeting obesity will mean fewer 'sick' people suffering from NCDs. This, in turn, will automatically reduce the demand for healthcare infrastructure and ease the strain on our clinicians. It will allow healthcare funds to be diverted to other 'prevention' areas, thus helping further alleviate the pressure on our already overburdened public healthcare systems. Most importantly, it will afford those formerly obese a more comfortable, high-quality life.

Zero Diseases to Zero Mortality

Imagine a world where a cure for the deadliest diseases has been found and where we have achieved the goal of zero diseases. No more a world with pandemics, superbugs and mutating viruses, this would be nirvana.

The discovery of vaccines has been one of the greatest success stories in eradicating several diseases and bringing their incidence to zero. For instance, smallpox was one of the deadliest diseases in history, killing around 30 per cent of humans who got infected with the virus, and leaving many with chronic illnesses. Edward Jenner created the first vaccine for smallpox in 1796 but it was only in the 1980s that WHO declared the disease to be eradicated, globally. Another disease that has been eradicated, although not in humans but in animals, is rinderpest.

Among other diseases that we have successfully eliminated include polio, measles, tetanus, hepatitis B, mumps, chickenpox and, more recently, malaria. It is important, however, to note that these diseases have been eliminated, not eradicated. Eradication refers to the incidence of the disease being permanently reduced to zero. On the other hand, elimination refers to a reduction in the occurrence of a disease and its restriction to a defined geographic area. With disease elimination, one still needs to put in place measures to prevent the re-emergence or transmission of the virus/bacterium.

Now we are close to another major feat—zero malaria. Malaria kills about 600,000 people a year, about 95 per cent of them in the African continent and about 80 per cent under the age of five.[14] A Zero Malaria Starts with Me campaign launched in Senegal in 2014 has since turned into a continent-wide movement. It is believed that a zero-malaria world is just a decade away, with a cheap jab now being mass produced by the Serum Institute of India with the Jenner Institute at Oxford University, UK.

Where we cannot completely eradicate diseases there is a case to aim for zero mortality, that is, reduce deaths from diseases.

The United Nations' 2030 Sustainable Development Goal #3 targets reducing premature mortality from NCDs by a third, lowering global maternal mortality rates, and ending preventable deaths of newborns and children under the age of five years. A similar goal is zero mortality from tuberculosis.

If we continue on this trajectory, we could, arguably, aim for the ultimate prize—zero mortality from preventable and treatable health conditions, including a majority of NCDs. Cancers, if diagnosed early, have a higher chance of being successfully treated, allowing patients to lead longer lives. Indeed, cardiovascular conditions and diabetes account for three of the top ten leading causes of mortality.[15]

Early diagnosis and prevention can lead to early targeted interventions, thus helping avert premature deaths due to diseases. This quest has led to the emergence of newer models such as full-body scan MRIs and wellness-focused services such as longevity clinics.

Such approaches that help reduce mortality from preventable and treatable diseases are likely to become commonplace, especially once the cost factor is addressed.

So, does this mean we are entering an era of immortality? Most research seems to indicate that cognitive and physical decline begins in our mid-twenties and continues to accelerate beyond that. Essentially, the biological processes that allow for growth and regeneration in our youth slow down and eventually stop, affecting our brain, muscles and organ systems. We call this self-destruct sequence 'aging'.

Over the course of human history, we have seen average life expectancy extend from twenty years in the neolithic era and twenty-eight years during ancient Rome, all the way up to forty-five years by the 1800s. At the start of the 1900s, life expectancy was only about fifty years, on average. However, major advances in medicine bumped up lifespans to sixty-five years by 1950, before ultimately settling around its present-day range of seventy-five to eighty years for most developed nations. Given medical advances and the potential for new breakthroughs, it is possible that one in six people alive in the developed world today will be centenarians and, some of them even supercentenarians.

Like the 80:20 rule, when it comes to life expectancy, two numbers to keep in mind are 80 and 120. The number 80 refers to what is considered the current average life expectancy, and 120 refers to the age of the oldest recorded human. The oldest woman recorded lived to the age of 122, and several individuals have reached the age of 115. It will not be too long before one of us reaches the age of 150.

Paradigm-shifting biomedical advances in the twenty-first century, once creatively imagined in film and literature, have elevated the concept of 'immortality' to a question of 'when' and not 'if'. Immortality involves a complex combination of gene-therapy techniques, tissue engineering and cybernetics used in concert to restore or replace failing organ systems.

From Transhumaism to Extropianism

My foresighting team tracks a trend called human augmentation where we explore how we are moving from transhumanism to

CHART 7.2: THE QUINTUPLE AIM OF HEALTHCARE

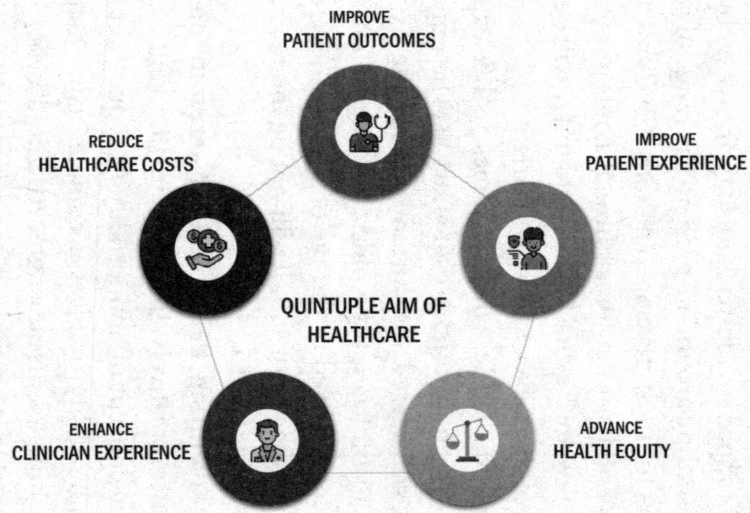

Source : Markets and Markets

CHART 7.3: FROM TRANSHUMANISM TO EXTROPIANISM : 10 WAYS HOW HUMANS WILL BE AUGMENTED

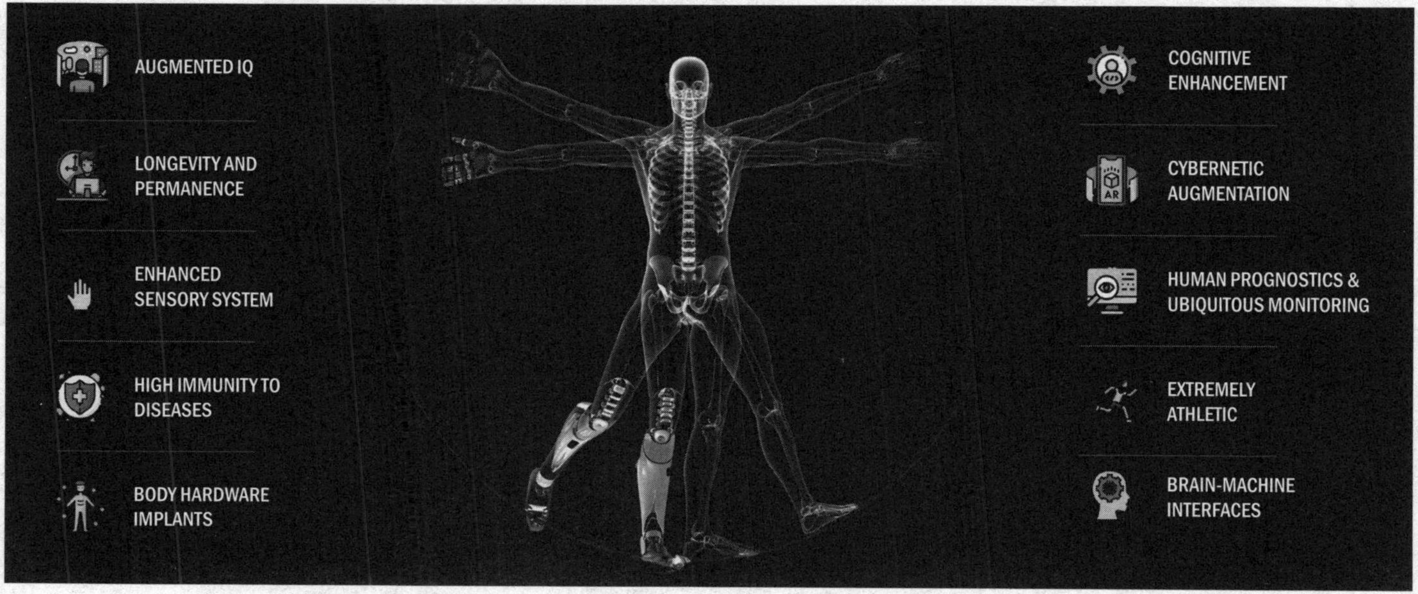

Source : Markets and Markets

extropianism. Chart 7.3 shows ten ways in which humans will be augmented in the future.

Extropianism, also referred to as the philosophy of extropy, is an 'evolving framework of values and standards for continuously improving the human condition'. Extropians believe that advances in science and technology will someday let people live indefinitely.[16]

This means, our bodies will be augmented through wearables that will surpass the fitness trackers of today. We will also see increased use of implants, ranging from brain microchips and neural lace to mind-controlled prosthesis and subdermal RFID chips that allow users to unlock doors or computer passwords with the wave of a hand. However, the most powerful body augmentation will come from biological augmentation as a result of increased insight into our genomes, advances in IVF technology that may allow us to select the most intelligent embryos, and powerful CRISPR gene-editing technology which may one day give us the ability to eliminate all heritable diseases.

Our thought processes will be faster and more transferable through both wearable and implantable brain-machine interfaces (BMIs). Mark Zuckerberg has described the following scenario: Today, when we share our vacation experiences, we upload photos and videos. With BMIs, I can share my full sensory and emotional vacation experience with friends and family. This could be the future of Facebook—sharing emotional experiences.

In the future, human enhancement will involve hardware, physical, intellectual, psychological and biological enhancements taking us closer to zero mortality.

While extending life indefinitely might not ever be realistically possible, we are likely to see significant progress in extending healthy life expectancy.

What Should We Expect in the Future of Healthcare

Healthcare is undergoing multiple, simultaneous transformations as an industry—a digital transformation, an equitable access transformation, an outcomes-focused clinical care for the diseased transformation, a preventable care-focused transformation and a sustainability-focused transformation. While these are all at various stages of maturity, their result will paint a vastly different picture of health and wellness for us in the future.

The entire 'patient healthcare experience' factor will change to 'a wellness experience' for us as health and wellness consumers. Care delivered 'anytime, anywhere', and a preventive focus will lead to a reduction in the overall prevalence of non-communicable, chronic disease in the long run. An improved focus on health, supported by technological advancements for reducing obesity, will also boost health outcomes. Overall, these will have varied implications for the pharma and life sciences sector, the medical devices sector, and the digital health sector in terms of what can be treated and what can be prevented.

The healthcare industry's future will be defined by the pursuit of zero, a transformative vision that will fundamentally reshape patient outcomes and care delivery. Striving for zero diseases, zero invasive surgery and zero patient wait times will represent not merely a quest for efficiency but a redefinition of healthcare itself. The emergence of net-zero hospitals will set new standards, minimizing environmental impacts while advancing cutting-edge care.

The shift from treatment to prevention, coupled with value-based medicine, will cause the traditional concept of hospitals to evolve, healthcare costs to fall and patients to be empowered to take control of their health with personalized, innovative solutions.

Harnessing advanced technologies and knowledge-sharing models, patient and clinician experiences will be revolutionized, while delivery will become more effective, equitable and tailored.

Ultimately, the vision of zero could even extend to conquering mortality itself—zero mortality—and challenge the very foundations of human existence.

8

INNOVATING TO ZERO IN THE TECHNOLOGY SECTOR

Technology and Artificial Intelligence and Its Role in Achieving Vision Zero

Hardly any discussion these days occurs without a mention of the transformative role of artificial intelligence (AI), and vision zero is no exception. AI refers to the simulation of human intelligence processes by machines. AI systems can transform how tasks are performed, particularly those that require human intelligence, such as visual perception, speech recognition, decision-making and language translation. AI has applications in various fields, ranging from healthcare and finance to transportation and entertainment. There has been even greater buzz about AI since the launch of ChatGPT in November 2022 and the kickstarting of the generative AI era. So how can AI help in achieving vision zero? Let's use the 'energy miracle' equation Bill Gates famously unveiled in his Ted Talk in 2010 to establish AI's likely impact on CO_2 emissions.

The Energy Miracle Equation:[1]

$CO_2 = P \times S \times E \times C$

where

CO_2 is the total carbon dioxide produced, which is believed to be the primary factor behind global warming

P is the total number of people in the world

S is the number of services consumed per person

E is the energy consumed to deliver a unit of service and

C is the CO_2 being put out per unit of energy

It doesn't require a PhD in mathematics to know that for carbon emissions to be zero, at least one of the factors in the equation needs to be zero. AI will have a far-reaching impact on all these factors through automation, simplification and elimination of specific tasks.

Through intelligent automation, AI can reduce the number of people required to perform mundane tasks and free them up for higher-level, more exciting work. Call-centre automation using AI agents is a typical example. The transformation of surveillance and monitoring-related tasks through computer vision is a more sophisticated example of how AI can reduce the number of services needed. We no longer need multiple security professionals driving around in specialized gas-guzzling SUVs or trucks to monitor our facilities, and intrusions or threats can be managed more on an exception basis. Full vehicle autonomy can potentially eliminate traffic accidents caused by human error. It can also reduce traffic congestion and driving-associated stress. Traffic violation-related fines come to mind immediately—imagine zero tickets or driving points. A vehicle doesn't need to be fully autonomous to achieve some of these benefits. Lane-departure and collision-alert systems already available in today's vehicles have started to make a difference. Since most of the autonomous vehicles currently available are electric or hybrid, they also have the potential to reduce emissions.

AI can also play a proactive role in the healthcare and transportation industries. The similarities in approaches and benefits of predicting health issues using AI with humans or vehicles are uncanny yet promising. Through the effective use of AI, the way healthcare providers can predict health issues and take proactive actions, transportation companies can also predict maintenance issues with vehicles and avoid costly breakdowns. Thus, AI could eliminate the number of services needed, increase the efficiency and profitability of operations and lower the environmental footprint of the healthcare and transportation industries.

This would not seem as far-fetched if we looked at some closer-to-home examples, like the AI-enabled Nest thermostat, which automatically adjusts home temperatures and optimizes energy consumption. The small smart device makes a big difference[2] by reducing greenhouse gas emissions while simultaneously reducing energy costs for homeowners. The impact of AI in lowering the environmental footprint is not limited to intelligent business-process automation, smart devices or autonomous vehicles. The more significant effect may come from generative AI, which can enable the creation of new products or services much more efficiently.

Generative AI tools comprising large language and image AI models have burst open a world of possibilities for the content-creation industry. Among them, automated content generation, improved quality, variety, accuracy and relevance of content, and enhanced content personalization. Generative AI models will leave no area which involves content creation—be it marketing, software, design, entertainment or interpersonal communications—untouched.

As shown in Chart 8.1, the generative AI technology roadmap will be as eventful, shifting focus from text and coding to images and video and, in due course, fully autonomous generative AI systems. An almost infinite number of use cases will emerge, with the sheer ubiquity and power of this technology underlining the need for strong ethical and regulatory safeguards.

From initially supporting in productivity gains in areas like content creation to realizing improved operational and resource efficiencies in fields like predictive maintenance to eventually assisting with breakthrough innovations in the space of drug and product development, the use cases of generative AI will only increase in tandem with their expanding capabilities (Chart 8.2).

In 2011, Marc Andreessen famously wrote, 'Software is eating the world.' Now, generative AI is getting ready to 'eat' software not by reducing or minimizing it but by generating it more efficiently. It will not remove the human element entirely, as someone still needs to validate that whatever code AI generates meets the business requirements; however, it may reduce the hours required to create a unit of code. Hopefully, all those efficiency gains will not just go directly to the bottom line. Some of this will lead to the creation of better products or services and ultimately make the digital world that humans rely on so heavily a better one. Generative AI assistants can be partners in product innovation and development processes. The enthusiasts can make a case that a generative AI quality-assurance assistant might have prevented the Crowdstrike issue, where a malformed code brought down business operations across the globe, making it the largest IT outage[3] in history. Overall, AI can play a significant role in achieving vision zero.

As we march toward the future, the role of technology becomes ever more critical—not just as an enabler of innovation but as the very foundation upon which industries, societies and individuals build a future of 'zero'. These ambitious visions are being driven forward by ICT innovations.

CHART 8.1: GENERATIVE AI TECHNOLOGY ROADMAP TILL 2030

	PRE-2020	2020	2022	2023*	2025**	2030***
TEXT	Spam detection translation basic Q&A	Basic copywriting first drafts	Longer forms second drafts	Vertical fine-tuning improves significantly (scientific paper, research articles, etc.)	Finals draft exceed average human baseline performance	Final drafts better than professional writers
CODE	1-line-auto-complete	Multi-line generation	Longer forms better accuracy	More language support more verticals	Text to product (draft)	Text to product (final) better than full-time developers
IMAGES			Art logos photography	Mock-ups (product design, architecture, etc.)	Final drafts (product design, architecture, etc.)	Finals drafts better than professional artists, designers and photographers
VIDEO/3D/GAMING			First attempts at 3D/video models	Basic/first draft videos and 3D files	Second drafts	AI roblox video games and movies offer high personalization

Initiation   Development   Commercialization

SHORT-TERM (2023-2025)*

- Improvements in Generative Adversarial Networks (GANs)
- Advancements in language modeling
- Increased use of Generative AI in creative industries
- Integration of Generative AI in Productivity Tools

MID-TERM (2026-2028)**

- Advances in meta-learning and few-shot learning techniques
- Development of Generative AI systems that can learn from multi-modal data
- Improvements in Generative AI-based language translation and localization

LONG-TERM (2029-2030)***

- The emergence of fully autonomous Generative AI systems
- Increased use of Generative AI in scientific research
- Advances in Generative AI ethics and regulation

Source: Secondary Research and MarketsandMarkets Analysis

CHART 8-2: GENERATIVE AI USE CASES FOR SECTORS
FROM SMALL PRODUCTIVITY GAINS, TO LARGE EFFICIENCY IMPROVEMENT AND EVENTUALLY TO INNOVATION

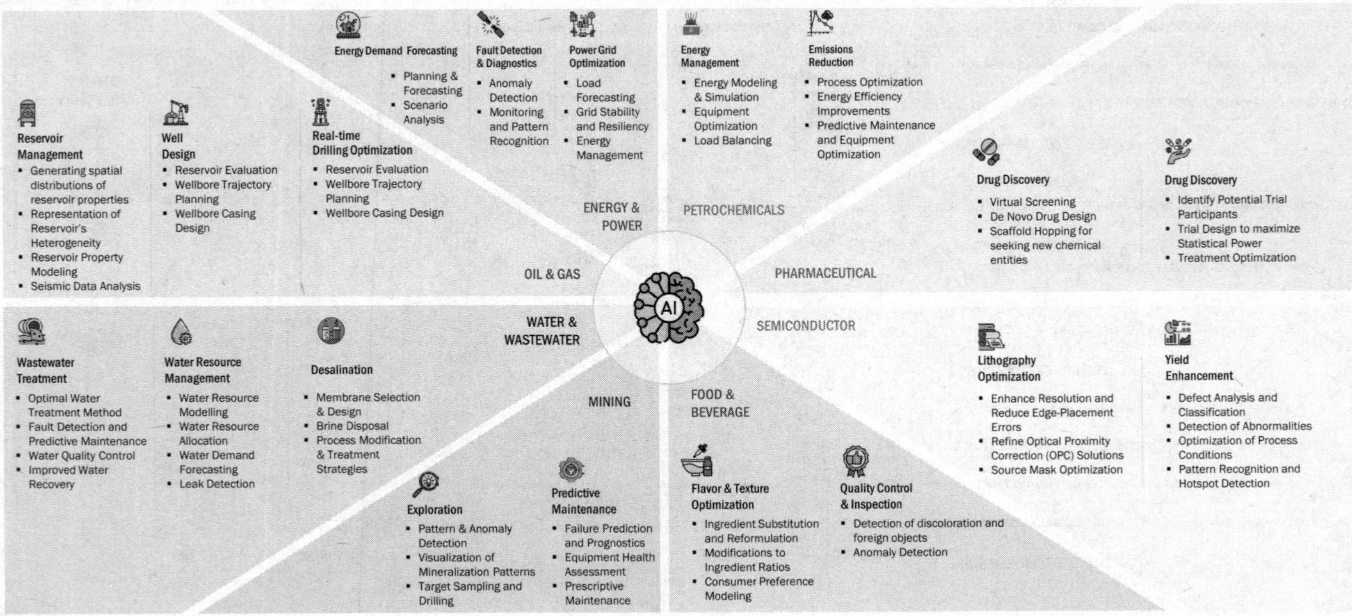

Source: MarketsandMarkets Analysis

Take the concept of 'zero blind spots'. As network technologies advance, we will move towards a world where connectivity is constant and ubiquitous—whether you're on land, at sea or in the air. Seamless handoffs between cellular, satellite and WiFi networks will ensure that you remain connected no matter where you go. Zero blind spots means that whether you're indoors, deep underground in a subway, flying high up in a plane or in the remotest of regions, at least one type of network will always be available. Companies like SpaceX's Starlink and OneWeb are already paving the way for satellite connectivity that can cover vast stretches of land and sea, while telecoms roll out 5G and 6G networks in the future to ensure high-speed terrestrial coverage. For instance, Starlink has launched over 6,300 satellites in orbit till date while it has approval from the US Federal Communications Commission (FCC) to launch a total of 12,000 satellites.[4] SpaceX is already trying to seek permission to launch an additional 30,000 Starlink satellites.[5] On the other hand, OneWeb's collaboration with global telecom operators like Orange is further closing connectivity gaps, targeting rural and remote areas previously left behind.[6]

This confluence of connectivity technologies brings us closer to 'zero digital divide'—a future where digital services are accessible to everyone, anywhere, regardless of geography. By eliminating blind spots, we can bridge the gap between the connected and the disconnected, offering digital services to underserved communities and ensuring equal access to education, healthcare and economic opportunities.

But connectivity alone won't suffice. The future we're imagining demands more than just ubiquitous access; it requires intelligent systems that operate without constraints. Enter the vision of zero AI processing constraints. In today's world, AI workloads are already split between devices and the cloud. Apple, for example, sends more intensive AI tasks to the cloud through its Private Cloud Compute,[7] while simpler tasks are processed locally on devices like the iPhone 16. This hybrid model works well, but it is only the beginning. In the future, AI processing will happen dynamically across devices, edge computing systems and cloud infrastructure with zero perceptible difference to the user. This would mean that whether you're interacting with AI on a mobile device, a smart home assistant or a complex industrial system, the processing happens wherever it is most efficient without the user even being aware of it. Thus, the constraints imposed by device limitations, bandwidth or computational power will be irrelevant. AI will seamlessly switch between local and cloud-based processing, creating a world where zero delays and zero limitations will define the user experience.

As these futuristic technologies become a reality, the next transformative step lies in embracing zero-friction business models, where in the not-too-distant future, the technological barriers that prevent enterprises and entrepreneurs from scaling their business ideas globally could disappear entirely. No-code platforms like Shopify already allow anyone to set up a functional e-commerce website in minutes, but this is just the start. As AI-driven software development matures, we will see the emergence of zero software development—a state where AI-driven development platforms enable anyone to create a fully functional digital product (whether a website, a mobile app or an enterprise solution) without needing coding skills. Take, for example, Devin, which is touted as the world's first fully autonomous AI software engineer. Developed by California-based start-up Cognition AI, Devin can plan and execute complex engineering tasks requiring thousands of decisions. Its real-world software engineering performance was tested on a coding benchmark (SWE-bench) and Devin came out with flying colours—it was at least 3X better than the previous 'state-of-the-art' model.[8]

But that's not the end of the story. Now, imagine layering generative AI on top of these advancements, turning this vision into a reality where ChatGPT–like AI systems function as full-fledged, real-time software engineers that can develop, troubleshoot and even deploy code. Amazon recently shared that its generative-AI assistant Amazon Q Developer, which is capable of writing code, testing, debugging, understanding existing code, finding security vulnerabilities, implementing new features, among others, helped the company to save over 4,500 developer-years resulting in $260 million in annual cost savings.[9]

At the core of these zero-friction business models will be the hyperscalers, acting as the final piece of the puzzle by offering seamless infrastructure management. Global cloud providers like AWS, Microsoft Azure and Google Cloud will provide zero infrastructure management, meaning all the computing, storage and security resources needed to scale business ideas will be managed automatically without the need to have an internal IT function. Therefore, zero-friction business models will ensure that innovation becomes the only currency for success. With technology as a commodity, available to anyone at any scale, competition will boil down to the originality and impact of the ideas themselves. This democratization of innovation will allow individuals and start-ups to challenge even the largest tech behemoths, without being constrained by infrastructure or development hurdles.

Looking deeper into the future of hyperscalers, we come to the concept of 'zero interruptions'. Today's cloud providers already offer impressive uptime guarantees, but the future holds even greater promise with the advent of AI-driven, self-healing networks. Companies like IBM[10] and Equinix[11] are leading the charge, developing networks that predict and fix issues autonomously. These systems monitor performance in real time, analyse traffic patterns and apply corrections without human intervention.

In this future, self-healing networks will ensure that critical industries—such as healthcare and autonomous vehicles—experience zero disruptions. For example, IBM's networks use AI to predict failures and reroute traffic before outages occur, while Equinix leverages digital twins to optimize network performance continuously. This could mean, for example, in healthcare, robotic systems like Intuitive Surgical's da Vinci[12] would maintain real-time connectivity for remote surgeries, ensuring that critical procedures are never disrupted. The vision of zero interruptions ensures that services, applications and systems will continue seamlessly, no matter the technical challenges or failures.

Alongside this, we will also witness the rise of zero distance from data. Edge computing is already enabling faster processing by bringing data closer to where it's needed, reducing latency and ensuring quicker responses. Today, hyperscaler solutions like AWS Wavelength[13] and Microsoft Azure Private Multi-Access Edge Compute (MEC)[14] are integrating edge computing with cloud infrastructure to deliver low-latency services across industries. These systems already ensure real-time processing for applications like smart manufacturing, AI-powered logistics and others.

But the future will take this to new heights. Hyperscalers, in partnership with edge-computing systems, will ensure that data and decision-making are always within reach, whether you're running a massive industrial operation or managing real-time AI assistants. This vision of zero distance from data ensures that decisions are made instantly, with no delay between data generation and actionable insights. In this future, businesses will operate at the speed of thought, eliminating bottlenecks and processing delays. From factories powered by AI-driven robots to real-time healthcare diagnostics, the ability to make split-second decisions with zero distance to data will redefine industries.

Looking even further ahead, the future will be defined by zero physical devices. As augmented reality (AR), virtual reality (VR) and brain-computer interfaces (BCIs) evolve, the need for traditional devices like smartphones, laptops and even wearable tech will diminish. Consider Elon Musk's BCI startup, Neuralink, that has already implanted the first human with a brain chip and the patient is able to control a computer mouse using their thoughts.[15] Recently, Neuralink implanted its device in a second patient and aims to further implant eight more patients in 2024 as part of its clinical trials.[16]

In this future, physical devices as we know them will disappear, replaced by zero-touch interfaces—voice commands, gestures and even neural signals like the ones from Neuralink that interact directly with digital environments.

In addition to BCIs, technologies like Microsoft's Mesh for Teams[17] and Apple's ARKit[18] are bringing us closer to a world where immersive interactions and zero-touch environments will be as intuitive as an in-person conversation. All interactions will happen in immersive environments, where hardware is invisible, and the digital world is seamlessly integrated with our physical surroundings. Zero physical devices could fundamentally change how we interact with the digital world, freeing us from the limitations of screens, keyboards and handheld gadgets.

If we go further into horizon 3, the Tech industry, in my opinion, is just facing the tip of the iceberg when it comes to disruption. Quantum computing is expected to be a game changer and it, in my opinion, is just around the corner. One could categorize

Quantum computing use cases into four key types, as I learnt in a recently held workshop in Germany by T-Systems:

1. Optimization, for example with supply chains
2. Chemistry simulation
3. Supporting machine learning which will immensely increase efficiency
4. Decryption/encryption—cryptography using quantum computing has already kicked off

Worrying as with the fourth use case, we will see in future 'quantum warfare' where the use of quantum both in defense and security will be profound and can be deadly.

In my opinion, countries will need to invest in a quantum ecosystem to protect but also benefit from this game-changing technology.

Conclusion

The potential of technology to innovate to zero is lightening workloads, enhancing efficiencies and transforming experiences in ways that once seemed unbelievable.

In healthcare, AI copilots have become game-changers for doctors, pharmacists and nurses buried hitherto in a sea of paperwork and patient data. AI assistants now fetch patient information at the click of a button. They summarize everything from medication lists to allergy histories, flag potential drug interactions and even check if medications are covered by insurance. AI is helping draft medical reports and ensuring smooth shift handovers. All this means healthcare workers have more time to focus on what truly matters—patient care.

In education, new technologies are making traditional classrooms obsolete. Professors are using generative AI to turn online lectures into textbooks. Students, with their diverse learning styles, can now choose to read, watch or even use mind maps to absorb information. Digital chatbots are also popping up, quickly and efficiently handling everything from IT assistance to course registration queries. This frees educators from performing routine bureaucratic and administrative tasks and allows them the time to engage more meaningfully and productively with students.

Earlier in this chapter, I talked about how generative AI tools had opened up new possibilities for the content-creation industry. Indeed, AI has no off-switch when it comes to creativity. In this context, I think of zero-effort writing, where an author plagued by writer's block simply suggests the plot of their novel to an AI assistant and proceeds to have a perfectly structured manuscript, complete with witty dialogue and an airtight plot, at their disposal within seconds—a literary masterpiece created with zero hours of agonizing rewrites. All I will add here is that it took me over two years, several sleepless nights and multiple drafts to finalize this book, so it was anything but zero effort and zero rewrites for me!

How about a vision of zero frustration with tech support? I often picture calling my internet provider and, instead of navigating a labyrinth of automated menus, being greeted by an AI with the calm, helpful patience of a Zen master. No more escalating my problem up a chain of supervisors but having AI solve my issue instantaneously.

To all this discussion about technology and vision zero, might I add a personal anecdote about how it is revolutionizing the customer experience? Last year, I finally decided it was time to give the gym another go. As a prelude to my physical exertions,

I turned to an online AI assistant seeking advice on appropriate gym wear. And AI worked its magic. Within seconds, I was pointed toward a sleek pair of joggers, a moisture-wicking tee and some trendy sneakers. And just like that, what would have been a frustrating search for random (and, I am sure, completely outdated) gym clothes turned into a personal styling session. The best part? No endless scrolling, no filters, just the perfect look delivered instantly. AI didn't just save my workout, it saved my style.

In short, rapid leaps in AI, connectivity and cloud infrastructure are offering opportunities to rethink how we approach innovation across sectors. From improving operational efficiencies to enabling breakthrough innovations in drug development and product design, generative AI and other emerging technologies are reshaping how we solve complex challenges. They are creating a world where barriers such as limited access, delays and computational constraints no longer hold us back, allowing us to aim for zero inefficiencies across industries.

The promise of zero blind spots through ubiquitous connectivity and zero digital divide as access to technology becomes universal is transforming how individuals and businesses engage with the world. The potential of zero-friction business models, zero-distance from data and zero physical devices is equally exciting. Hyperscalers like AWS and Microsoft Azure that offer seamless support—zero interruptions—are allowing global enterprises and entrepreneurs alike to scale their innovations without worrying about infrastructure management.

Such technology-driven shifts are ensuring that the only limit to success will be the power of innovation itself.

9

INNOVATING TO ZERO IN OUR SOCIETY

Innovating to zero could mean different things to different people. Whether as individuals and communities or governments and corporations, whether driven by business objectives or non-profit priorities—irrespective of what it is we do and who it is we are—this vision touches every one of us. In this, it addresses the interconnected social, environmental and economic challenges we face with implications for the overall harmony of life on earth. As these challenges become more acute, the need to find holistic, forward-looking zero-vision solutions is becoming ever more urgent.

Smart Cities and the Zero Vision

The European Commission defines a smart city as 'a place where traditional networks and services are made more efficient with the use of digital solutions for the benefit of its inhabitants and business'. This means that a smart city goes beyond merely leveraging digital technologies to reduce resource consumption and emissions. It integrates smarter urban transport, upgraded water supply, efficient waste management and innovative methods for lighting and heating buildings. Additionally, it envisions a city that is more interactive, responsive to its residents' needs, promotes safer public spaces and caters to the challenges of an aging population.

The concept of a smart city isn't just about technology—it's about improving the overall quality of life. The IMD Smart City Index Report 2023 ranks Zurich and Oslo at the top of its list, positions they have held since 2019. Other cities like Canberra, Copenhagen, London, Singapore and Stockholm also feature prominently.[1] Notably, these cities are evaluated based on key indicators such as health and safety, mobility, opportunities for employment and education, governance and quality of life, including green spaces and cultural activities. Ultimately, a true smart city prioritizes people—using technology as a tool to create inclusive, diverse and sustainable urban environments.

Central to the vision of smart cities is innovating to zero. This philosophy focuses on achieving zero emissions and creating cities that are carbon-neutral or even carbon-negative.[2] To accomplish this, smart cities will need to implement smart solutions that encompass multiple sectors—energy, buildings, transportation, industry, healthcare and governance—each working synchronously towards a future with zero environmental impact.

Smart Energy: Building the Foundation for Zero Emissions

In terms of smart energy, technologies like smart metres, which track energy usage, help consumers optimize their consumption patterns. Smart grids, which manage the storage and distribution of renewable energy, ensure a steady and reliable power supply even when renewable sources are intermittent. Supporting infrastructure for renewable energy, such as wind and solar, are key components in reducing overall energy consumption per capita.

In many Smart Cities, we are already seeing a push toward Zero Energy Buildings (ZEB). These structures employ Building Energy Management Systems (BEMS) to monitor and minimize energy use, incorporating energy-efficient architectural designs and intelligent systems like smart heating, ventilation and air conditioning (HVAC), and automated lighting controls. By integrating renewable energy sources—such as solar panels or onsite energy generation—these buildings significantly lower greenhouse gas emissions while promoting sustainable living. Climate-responsive architecture further enhances energy efficiency by adapting to local environmental conditions, ensuring minimal energy waste.

Smart Mobility: Moving Toward Zero Emissions Transport

Cities worldwide are adopting low or zero emission vehicles (ZEVs) powered by electric powertrains or hydrogen fuel cells. The rise of electric vehicles (EVs) has paved the way for more sustainable personal and public transport. Additionally, integrated and multimodal transport systems, for both personal and freight purposes, are making mobility smarter. By linking different modes of transport—such as buses, trains and ride-sharing services—cities can strengthen seamless, data-driven transit networks that reduce the carbon footprint of travel.

For a truly sustainable transport system, smart cities need to develop the infrastructure to encourage ZEVs, including extensive charging networks for EVs and hydrogen fuelling stations. In tandem, cities must create the infrastructure for eco-friendly transportation modes like cycling and walking. Supporting the expanded use of car-sharing and ride-hailing services will promote the adoption of alternatives to private vehicle ownership. These efforts align with the broader goal of integrating green principles into every aspect of urban infrastructure, creating cities that are not only smart but also sustainable.

Smart Manufacturing: Innovating Production Processes

Smart cities can transform the industrial sector, with smart manufacturing leading the way. In this approach, factories will utilize cutting-edge technologies such as augmented reality (AR), robotics, automation, 3D simulation, machine learning, cloud computing and artificial intelligence (AI) to streamline production processes. Smart factories will monitor and optimize manufacturing performance, resulting in increased productivity, reduced waste and higher efficiency. These innovations will allow for zero defects and zero downtime, significantly enhancing the sustainability of industrial operations.

Advanced Technologies: The Backbone of Zero-Carbon Cities

At the heart of smart cities' drive to achieve zero emissions are advanced technologies like AI, machine learning, digital twins, big-data analytics, machine-to-machine (M2M) communications, high-speed broadband and 5G connectivity. These digital tools will allow cities to optimize resource consumption, track environmental performance and create data-driven governance models. Digital twins—virtual replicas of physical environments—will enable city planners to simulate and evaluate the impacts of various initiatives before implementation. By providing detailed insights into the effects of different 'zero' based policies, these technologies can ensure that smart city strategies are both efficient and effective. They will help shape meaningful policy and governance while supporting affordable, accessible and quality service delivery. In addition to technological advances, smart cities will need to endorse new business models like circular economies that reinforce responsible consumption and production through a focus on recycling, reuse, waste reduction, and resource conservation and optimization.

Smart Governance and Smart Citizens: A Collaborative Effort

None of these innovations will be possible without the engagement of both governments and citizens. Smart governance will involve creating policies that incentivize sustainable practices across sectors, from corporations to local communities. By offering financial rewards, regulatory support or tax breaks, governments will motivate businesses to adopt greener technologies and citizens to make more sustainable lifestyle choices.

Equally important are smart citizens—individuals who actively participate in the city's sustainability efforts. Whether it's cycling to work or adopting pay-as-you-throw waste systems, citizens will have a critical role to play in reducing waste and energy consumption. In Germany, for example, such waste-management strategies have significantly decreased landfill usage, bringing communities closer to the goal of zero waste.

Smart Cities: A Holistic Approach to Innovating to Zero

Ultimately, smart cities represent more than just technological advancements; they embody a new way of thinking about urban living. By integrating the principles of sustainability, innovation and inclusivity, smart cities can create environments that are beneficial for people, the planet and profits. The vision of innovating to zero unites these goals, fostering cities that are smarter, greener and more resilient for the future. Smart truly is the new green.

Kicking Off a New Era in Sustainable Sports

The match between Tottenham Hotspur vs Chelsea in September 2021 stood out for reasons other than proceedings on the pitch. As the world's first elite-level net-zero carbon football match, it aimed to highlight climate change and 'spur' fans to adopt small, eco-friendly habits. The event introduced innovative strategies, setting a new benchmark for integrating sustainability into sports across all levels. It demonstrated how sports can lead climate action efforts.

A Best-Practices Case Study

Tottenham Hotspur: Game Zero

In September 2021, Tottenham Hotspur Football Club made history, not just in the Premier League but on the global stage, by hosting the world's first net-zero carbon football match at an elite level.[3] Dubbed 'Game Zero', this groundbreaking event was held at the Tottenham Hotspur Stadium during a match against Chelsea. But the real victory was off the pitch, as the club showcased a pioneering approach to drastically reducing the environmental impact of major sporting events.

Game Zero was the culmination of a collaborative effort involving Tottenham Hotspur, Sky Sports, and independent carbon experts from RSK and Natural Capital Partners. The goal? To go beyond the immediate objective of hosting a single net-zero carbon football game and create a replicable model for how sports clubs and organizations worldwide could take meaningful action on environmental sustainability.

It started with establishing a baseline of carbon emissions for a typical match day at Tottenham Hotspur Stadium. Armed with this data, the team was able to obtain a clear picture of the emissions involved, allowing them to strategically target areas where reductions could be made. Any remaining unavoidable emissions were offset through a community reforestation project in East Africa.

The strategies implemented for Game Zero were as innovative as they were effective. The players didn't just arrive in style—they arrived sustainably, on buses powered by green biodiesel, slashing squad travel emissions by over 80 per cent. Fans got in on the action too, walking a collective 36,000 miles and driving 225,000 miles in electric or hybrid vehicles to attend the match. Inside the stadium, everything from heating to cooking was powered entirely by renewable energy. Catering services offered locally sourced, sustainable food, with a whopping 94 per cent increase in sales of vegetarian and plant-based meals from the previous match. Even Sky Sports, which covered the game, played its part by reducing the emissions of its production team by 70 per cent.

Turning Green

Tottenham Hotspur's leadership in environment responsibility is well-established within the Premier League, earning it recognition as the league's greenest club by the UN-backed Sport Positive Summit. Across its operations, Tottenham Hotspur has implemented a comprehensive range of sustainable practices. The stadium is powered entirely by renewable electricity, resulting in Zero Scope 2 emissions. Energy efficiency measures, such as LED lighting and high-efficiency systems, further enhance sustainability. The club operates a zero-to-landfill waste-management programme, ensuring that no waste is sent to landfills, with clear recycling instructions provided to fans. Single-use plastics have been significantly reduced across the stadium, with recyclable packaging and wooden cutlery being standard practice.

The club's training centre features an organic kitchen garden, wildlife ponds and green roofs, all designed to enhance biodiversity. These initiatives reflect the club's holistic approach to sustainability, extending beyond the stadium to every aspect of its operations.

The club's dedication to environmental stewardship is underscored by its participation in global initiatives like the UN Race to Zero, where it has committed to halving its carbon emissions by 2030 and achieving net-zero carbon by 2040. Tottenham Hotspur is also a signatory to the UN Sports for Climate Action Framework, which calls on sports organizations to address their impact on climate change. The club is a founding member of Count Us In, a global movement aimed at mobilizing one billion people to take action on climate change.

This commitment to sustainability has earned the club the prestigious ISO 20121 certification, awarded by the British Standards Institution (BSI).[4] This certification serves as a guide for sustainable event management, steering organizations to seamlessly integrate sustainability into every facet of their operations.

As one of the Premier League's greenest clubs, the club's commitment to sustainability—'Passionate About Our

Planet'—is an ongoing journey. Through initiatives like Game Zero, Tottenham Hotspur is not only setting new standards in sustainability but also proving that even the largest sporting events can achieve meaningful environmental change.

To learn more, I spoke with Marcus Parry, sustainability manager at Tottenham Hotspur: 'We have a clear decarbonization plan, "Passionate About Our Planet", focusing on four key areas: fan travel, procurement, business travel and energy use. Fan travel is the biggest contributor, accounting for 50 per cent of the club's carbon footprint, while procurement contributes 37 per cent, energy 6 per cent and business travel 4 per cent. The club is working with Schneider Electric to optimize energy use.'

He added, 'Tottenham has a sustainability working group that meets quarterly to assess progress. The current focus is on improving the accuracy of emissions data, particularly from procurement, which largely comes from catering (30 per cent of procurement). The club is aiming to move from spend-based to activity-based reporting, such as tracking the amounts of meat and vegetables sold to refine emissions estimates.'

'Additionally, Tottenham is collaborating with UEFA to align on emissions reporting,' Parry said. 'While only a few football clubs have started reporting their emissions, Tottenham has reported its full carbon footprint for three years and is working to enhance this reporting.'

'The club has received permission to host thirty additional events, which brings the total to sixty events annually, including NFL games and music concerts,' he added. 'Tottenham is focusing on ensuring these events are sustainable by pressuring third-party vendors to meet environmental standards.'

Beyond sustainability, the club is committed to social responsibility. Elaborating on this, Tony Stevens, head of public relations, noted, 'Tottenham is actively involved in regenerating its local area, one of the poorest in London. It supports employment, health and education, including funding a local Sixth Form college and works closely with food banks to combat food poverty by redirecting surplus food from events to charitable causes. With over 100 million followers, the club recognizes its responsibility to lead by example in both sustainability and community development.'

So while Tottenham is all about the positive outcomes related to innovating to zero, both gentlemen concurred that they did not want to see a zero on the scoreboard!

And while it is hard to admit this as an Arsenal fan, when it comes to saving the planet, the Spurs have us beaten 1-0. Our rivalry on the pitch will continue, but off it, I'll concede—Tottenham have scored a big win for sustainability. Just don't expect me to cheer them on at the North London Derby!

FIGURE 10.1 : Zero In Our Society	
Zero carbon emissions	Zero education achievement gap
Zero waste	Zero plastic waste
Zero hunger	Zero urban sprawl
Zero homelessness	Zero energy poverty
Zero traffic deaths	Zero food deserts
Zero water pollution	Zero greenhouse gas emissions
Zero unemployment	Zero opioid epidemic
Zero income inequality	Zero child poverty
Zero air pollution	Zero corruption
Zero crime	Zero carbon buildings
Zero racial disparities	

Innovating to Zero and the UN's Sustainable Development Goals

'Innovating to zero' represents a bold vision for the future, a pathway to achieving the United Nations' seventeen Sustainable Development Goals (SDGs).[5] At its core, this concept drives innovation towards eliminating the world's most pressing challenges—zero poverty, zero hunger, zero preventable deaths and zero inequality, among others. The urgency for sustainable solutions is paramount as the world grapples with climate change, economic instability and growing inequality. Mobilizing partnerships will be key to fostering peaceful, inclusive societies, building effective institutions, and restoring ecosystems and biodiversity. From transforming urban spaces to protecting marine environments, innovating to zero calls for concerted action across sectors.

The transition to sustainable cities and communities, along with resilient infrastructure, lies at the core of this vision. Sustainable consumption, climate resilience and mitigating environmental impacts will need to underpin global industrialization efforts. Ensuring access to modern, clean energy, and securing water resources will be vital components, alongside reducing inequalities both within and among countries. Moreover, advancing education through technology, empowering women to close the gender gap, and ensuring universal health access will be critical for fostering equity. Each of these goals is connected, reinforcing the need for a comprehensive, innovative approach to achieving economic inclusion and safeguarding the future of our planet using a vision-zero approach. To these seventeen SDGs and how vision zero can catalyse them, I have added some of my own.

Zero Poverty

The combined forces of the pandemic, climate change and conflict have driven millions back into poverty, with even affluent nations grappling with the issue. According to the World Bank, almost 700 million people around the world live today in extreme poverty—they subsist on less than $2.15 per day, the extreme poverty line.[6] Today, 30 million children live in poverty across the world's wealthiest countries. Without substantial change, it's estimated that 575 million people—an estimated 7 per cent of the global population—could still be living in extreme poverty by 2030.[7]

To achieve zero poverty, we will need large-scale innovation that fosters inclusive economic growth and reaches the most marginalized. Digital technologies, mobile banking, microfinancing and skills training will offer a lifeline to underserved populations, providing them with access to financial services and economic opportunities. Investments in renewable energy will create sustainable jobs and lower living costs, helping lift communities out of poverty. Collaboration between governments and the private sector will be critical in developing social safety nets, affordable housing and digital-inclusion programmes. By innovating to zero, we will be able to ensure that resources are distributed more equitably, basic needs like food, shelter, and clothing are met, and individuals are given the tools to improve their quality of life.

Zero Hunger

'Put simply: hunger and poverty are intertwined. We need to take them on and work hard to rid our world of both.'

— Ajay Banga, World Bank Group President

The idea of zero hunger is second in the UN's Sustainable Development Goals. According to the UN, in 2022, an estimated 735 million people faced conditions of chronic hunger, 2.4 billion people confronted moderate to severe food insecurity, 148 million children had stunted growth, 45 million children under the age of five were affected by wasting even as 37 million were deemed overweight. By 2030, over 600 million people globally will be hungry.[8] This has deep implications for health and education, social and economic development, and serves to emphasize the tremendous challenge of achieving zero hunger.

The world produces enough food to feed everyone, yet 828 million people go hungry every day. Food insecurity has been worsened by conflict, climate change and inequality, with vulnerable communities bearing the brunt. Unless current trends change, the number of people facing hunger is set to surpass 600 million by 2030. Rising food prices are a particular threat to low-income nations, where malnutrition severely hinders development, leaving millions of children stunted or wasted.

What will it take to get to zero hunger? At the most fundamental level, it will require policy coordination, collective action from governments, NGOs and communities, and initiatives in the agriculture, healthcare and education sectors. It will require support for sustainable farming practices, the judicious use of new productivity-enhancing agricultural technologies, less food waste, and more equitable food-distribution systems. It will require community empowerment, improved food security and healthcare, and better nutrition, especially for vulnerable populations. It will require climate-smart solutions like agroforestry, precision agriculture and crop biotechnology that can boost food production while reducing environmental impact. It will embrace innovative approaches such as vertical farming and lab-grown food that can revolutionize urban food systems, making fresh produce more accessible and reducing reliance on traditional farming. Additionally, reducing food waste and improving warehousing and distribution networks will ensure food security, while supporting equitable growth. These innovations, driven by sustainable and efficient practices, can pave the way towards a future free from hunger.

A Best-Practices Case Study

Britannia: Biscuits and Zero Malnutrition

Britannia, an Indian multinational food company, has made 'zero malnutrition' a core goal, not just through CSR but by developing iron-enriched biscuits that have become bestsellers. Their public–private partnership initiative has combated malnutrition among millions of children in India. Britannia's success shows how companies can thrive by embracing an innovating to zero vision.

Combating Malnutrition one Biscuit at a Time

A recently published study in the peer-reviewed JAMA Network Open journal found that India ranks as having the third highest percentage of 'zero-food' children. The prevalence of zero-food children, that is, children between six and twenty-three months old who did not consume any animal milk, formula, or solid or semisolid food within twenty-four hours before being surveyed, in India, declined from 20.0 per cent (95 per cent CI: 19.3 per cent–20.7 per cent) in 1993 to 17.8 per cent (95 per cent CI: 17.5 per cent–18.1 per cent).[9]

India's nutritional crisis, particularly among children, is grave, given that about 12.9 per cent of the country's population falls below the poverty line (World Bank 2021). With a population of around 1.4 billion in 2022, that equates to about 182 million people who suffer from malnutrition.

India's National Family Health Survey (NFHS-5), conducted in 2019–20, highlighted a decline in the nutritional status of children under the age of five. The first phase of the survey, which covered seventeen states revealed that stunting as well as the incidence of underweight children had increased in eleven states, while severe wasting had risen in thirteen states.[10]

Malnutrition and the consequences of vitamin and mineral deficiencies could cost as much as 2–3 per cent of a country's GDP in terms of healthcare, with additional costs linked to low productivity estimated at up to 3 per cent of GDP for some countries. Underscoring this link, Reserve Bank of India's former governor Raghuram Rajan noted that addressing problems like malnutrition, which affected the country's most important asset, viz. human capital, was a critical prerequisite to India becoming a developed nation.[11]

The United Nations' Food and Agriculture Organization (FAO), *Asia and the Pacific—Regional Overview of Food Security and Nutrition 2023*, highlights hunger and under nutrition faced by a large section of the world's population, especially in South Asia which has 85 per cent of undernourished people, equating to around 314 million people.[12] Particularly worrisome are malnutrition rates among children with extreme hunger resulting in stunting and wasting.

The Global Nutrition Report 2022 indicated that addressing child wasting remains an ongoing challenge in India, with 17.3 per cent of children under five years of age being affected.[13] The Global Hunger Index (GHI) 2023 reported that India has one of the highest rates of child wasting globally, at 18.7 per cent, highlighting ongoing concerns around undernutrition. The report which studies four key indicators—undernourishment, child stunting, child wasting and child mortality—estimated 16.6 per cent of India's population as being undernourished.[14]

India's Global Hunger Index (GHI) score of 28.7 places it in the 'serious' hunger category, along with nations such as Pakistan (26.6), Afghanistan (30.6) and Sudan (27). The country's child wasting rate of 18.7 per cent is among the highest, exceeding rates in Yemen (14.4 per cent) and Sudan (13.7 per cent).

India ranked 111th out of 124 countries on the Global Hunger Index, following Pakistan (102nd), Bangladesh (81st), Nepal (69th) and Sri Lanka (60th). Additionally, among Indian women aged fifteen to twenty-four years, anaemia was observed at a rate of 58.1 per cent.

In short, malnutrition has been, and continues to be, a major challenge for India. Recognizing this, the government has been working towards zero malnutrition, reinforced by efforts from the private sector. One of the most successful public–private partnerships has been Britannia Industries' 'Zero Malnutrition' initiative for children.

Founded in 1892 in Kolkata (formerly Calcutta), Britannia is today one of India's biggest and most well-known food brands. In the 1980s, Britannia Industries Limited (BIL) crossed $25 million in revenues. It was rated amongst the top 300 small companies of the world by Forbes Global (2002) and recognized as India's Most Trusted Food Brand by The Economic Times (2007). Currently, Britannia has an annual revenue of over ₹165 billion with rural operations outperforming urban. In 2024, Britannia was recognized by KANTAR as the Most Chosen FMCG Brand #1 in 'OOH' and #2 in 'In-Home'.

Realizing the need to do something about the 40 per cent of children in India who were undernourished and the nearly 50 per cent of school-going children who were iron deficient (Assocham and EY study based on WHO 2015 data), Britannia embarked on an ambitious project aimed at developing a product that would provide a simple, cost-effective way to deliver nutrition. Focused R&D and multiple trials were conducted before Britannia zeroed in on the final product.

Guided by its vision of achieving zero malnutrition for millions of India's children, Britannia began delivering nutrition through iron-enriched biscuits. A collaborative effort between Britannia, the Naandi Foundation and the Global Alliance for Improved Nutrition (GAIN), this example of business innovation provided iron-enriched biscuits to school children.[15] In some cities, like Hyderabad, it was given as a supplement to state government-sponsored mid-day meal schemes. Initially, each child was given two iron-enriched biscuits on a twice-weekly basis. To ensure the long-term sustainability of this project, Britannia and Naandi conducted awareness-raising programmes among parents and educators emphasizing the importance of incorporating iron into one's diet.

Interestingly, the company's R&D team ensured that the cost of iron enrichment was offset by improving system efficiencies, thereby ensuring that the product remained affordable to consumers.

Initially, only the popular Tiger brand of biscuits were enriched. However, what started as a one-off experiment became a huge success. Britannia then decided to turn its attention to other products, and now many of its products, including bestselling biscuit brands like Marie Gold and Milk Bikis and more, as well as its Britannia Bread come enriched with essential nutrients.

The company did not just stop there. In 2010, it set up the Britannia Nutrition Foundation (BNF) with the vision of having a malnutrition-free India. BNF offers comprehensive programmes to manage undernutrition and iron-deficiency anaemia, addressing the nutrition requirements of severe and moderately acute malnutrition among children, adolescents and expectant/new mothers. Committed to 'breaking the intergenerational cycle of malnutrition', BNF has positively impacted over 230,000 people since its inception, with beneficiaries located in over 600 villages and slums spread across nine states.

To learn more about Britannia and its zero-malnutrition objective, I interviewed senior leader, Manjunath Desai, vice president, Consumer Insight, Media and Competitive Intelligence. While shedding light on Britannia's efforts in this area, Desai also spoke about a lesser-known aspect, that is, the development of a unique biscuit aimed at addressing malnutrition. This biscuit was not sold commercially but was specifically produced to help reduce anaemia and iron deficiency in children.

'Britannia's primary expertise was in the field of food and nutrition and its zero-malnutrition initiative was, therefore, a natural extension of this expertise. The company saw its efforts at developing a mineral-enriched product that it could make easily accessible to the people who most needed it.

Nutrition, or the lack thereof, was one of the more pressing issues that India faced, mostly in the form of malnutrition. The problem at whatever stage it might be—whether severely acute malnutrition, medium acute malnutrition or moderately acute malnutrition—was clearly and widely visible. Indeed, one didn't need any scientific measurement to determine in which of these categories a malnourished child fell, it was simply a matter of concluding that the child was malnourished, reflected in poor physical development, including stunting and other medical conditions.

For BNF, beyond the obvious lack of access was also the challenge of addressing the lack of understanding and knowledge about the critical role of iron in one's diet. So, in addition to helping children break free from the manacles of malnutrition, the company worked towards helping them stay that way, not only by giving them continuous support, but also by educating their families, equipping them to earn or by resource mobilization with the two-fold objective of, firstly, keeping children that had originally been helped to emerge out of the malnutrition bracket not relapse, and, secondly, ensuring that children who were otherwise healthy remained that way because anybody, including children who are not fed adequately and correctly for a period of time, can end up suffering from malnutrition.

In fact, it is not uncommon to find kids of relatively well-to-do families being anaemic and there being no knowledge that they are anaemic. Here, it's not just a function of diet, it is a function of lack of understanding.

So our biscuits enriched with iron came in as a real game changer when it came to combating anaemia for beneficiaries under BNF.'

Iron is necessary from a functional health perspective but what about from a taste perspective? Take, for instance, the Indian government's efforts to address the challenge of anaemia through iron-enriched rice under the National Food Security Act (NFSA). Media reports seem to indicate that this was met with a less-than-enthusiastic response because of the relatively unappetizing look, taste and feel of these iron-enriched grains.

While enriching biscuits with iron, therefore, Britannia had to deal with an undesirable sensory attribute of iron, that is, its taste. Rigorous R&D was required to make the biscuits palatable and not have children reject it because it tasted more like metal than a snack. In short, R&D faced a double challenge of, firstly, ensuring that there was adequate iron in the biscuit and, then again, ensuring that the presence of iron didn't alter the taste of a biscuit to the extent that it landed up uneaten. On both counts, Britannia succeeded.

Its zero-malnutrition initiative remains a benchmark in corporate social responsibility, in demonstrating how an 'iron' will can go a long way to combating endemic public health issues and sparking positive zero outcomes.

Zero Obesity

Malnutrition has two very different faces: extreme hunger and obesity. A recent report published in the *Lancet* medical journal made me clean out my junk-food cupboard. The report states that over one billion people around the world are now obese. Obesity rates among children and adolescents have quadrupled from 1990 to 2022, while obesity rates among adults have more than doubled. In 2022, 160 million (65 million girls and 94 million boys) were affected by obesity, compared to 31 million in 1990.

For adults, obesity rates spiked to 880 million in 2022 from 195 million in 1990.[16]

Obesity imposes a huge burden on society in multiple ways. They are associated with a wide range of noncommunicable diseases (NCDs) including diabetes, cancer, cardiovascular diseases, respiratory diseases and neurological disorders. These, in turn, put public healthcare systems under tremendous strain. In terms of its economic impacts, the obesity pandemic is projected to rack up an annual cost of $3 trillion by 2030 and more than $18 trillion by 2060. Tellingly, obesity is no longer a first-world problem of plenty. It now affects low- and middle-income countries, including lower socio-economic groups.

So how do we get to zero obesity? I think the first point to consider is that obesity with its attendant NCDs, is preventable and manageable. Given this, it will require multisectoral, multilevel, multistakeholder approaches. Individuals can overhaul their lifestyle and encourage positive behaviours—especially among young people—around healthy diets and eating behaviour, adequate and regular physical activity, proper rest, and mental and physical wellbeing. In short, incorporating preventative interventions at every stage of our life.

As the WHO says, 'Obesity is a societal rather than individual responsibility, with the solutions to be found through the creation of supportive environments and communities that embed healthy diets and regular physical activity as the most accessible, available and affordable behaviours of daily life.'[17] So, on the other side of the scale, the levying of higher 'fat' or 'sin' taxes on foods with higher salt, sugar and salt or legally mandating warning labels on unhealthy foods could reduce consumption of unhealthy food and, by extension, premature deaths linked to obesity.[18] How about motivating people to be healthy by offering subsidized gym memberships? What about lower insurance premiums for healthy lifestyles? Fad or not, functional foods, organic foods, and low-calorie and low-sugar foods are becoming popular. I mean, who would have ever imagined Coke coming up with zero-sugar drinks like Coke Zero? My vote goes to Brand Zero.

Zero Preventable Deaths

While global health systems have made notable progress in reducing child mortality and fighting diseases like HIV and malaria, the COVID-19 pandemic has reversed many of these hard-won gains. Millions missed out on vital immunizations, and preventable diseases, once under control, are resurfacing. Health systems worldwide are strained—many face chronic underfunding, inadequate infrastructure and lack of access to essential services. For example, every two minutes, a woman dies from preventable pregnancy-related causes,[19] underscoring the urgent need for better maternal care.

To truly achieve zero preventable deaths, we will need to rethink how healthcare is delivered. Innovation will be the key to this transformation. Telemedicine and digital health platforms are already bridging gaps in access, bringing healthcare to underserved communities, and lowering the cost of care. AI-driven diagnostics can revolutionize early detection of diseases, making healthcare more efficient and easing the burden on medical professionals. But technology alone isn't enough. We will need to expand access to affordable vaccines and treatments while strengthening healthcare infrastructure globally. Innovating to zero in health is about creating a system where high-quality, equitable care is accessible to everyone—regardless of where they live or their income level. By leveraging technology and fostering international collaboration, we will be able to eliminate health disparities and promote universal well-being.

Zero-Concept Hospitals and Net-Zero Healthcare

The COVID-19 pandemic was a stark reminder of how fragile our health systems can be. But it also showed us the power of innovation. The concept of zero can be applied across various aspects of healthcare. For instance, net-zero hospitals are emerging as models of sustainability, built to maximize energy efficiency and generate zero medical waste.[20] These facilities could serve as the foundation for a more sustainable healthcare ecosystem.

But the idea of zero extends beyond infrastructure—it touches the very core of patient care.

Zero-Concept Patients: A New Hope for Healthcare

For patients, the dream of zero takes on many forms. Imagine a world where invasive surgeries are no longer necessary, surgical errors are eradicated and lifestyle diseases are a thing of the past. With advances in medical technology, remote healthcare and preventative care, these goals are within reach. From the wider use of mobile and electronic health solutions to cutting-edge diagnostics, zero represents the hope for a future where health and wellness are prioritized. While the vision of zero diseases may seem idealistic, history shows us it's possible—just look at the near-eradication of polio in many regions.

Zero Healthcare Disparities: The Role of Smart Cities

Eliminating healthcare disparities is an essential part of the zero vision, and smart cities have a pivotal role to play in this effort. By expanding the use of digital health technologies, we will be able to improve healthcare access, monitor public-health trends and address disparities in real time. Telemedicine platforms, wearable health trackers and predictive modeling tools are all part of this future, enabling proactive, personalized healthcare management.

Achieving zero preventable deaths will take coordinated, global action. But through innovation, technology and a commitment to equitable care, it's a realizable future.

Zero Educational Inequality

Education remains the cornerstone of economic mobility, yet millions of children globally are still left behind. The COVID-19 pandemic caused widespread learning losses, with an estimated 84 million children at risk of staying out of school without further intervention. Many educational systems are not equipped to meet the demands of the global economy, especially in less-developed regions, where gender disparities, inadequate resources and insufficient infrastructure hinder progress.

At the heart of zero educational inequality will be improved accessibility to good quality, cost-effective education. Take the case of Japan[21] which has a 100 per cent enrollment rate in compulsory grades and—as a result—zero illiteracy.

As the digital divide in education deepens, the use of technologies to bridge the gap, expand educational access and extend digital literacy programmes to more people will become an increasingly critical aspect of both zero educational inequality and innovating-to-zero illiteracy. Eliminating educational inequality and illiteracy will require a bold embrace of technology. Digital tools can bring quality education to marginalized students through remote and hybrid learning models, expanding access to high-quality content even in resource-limited areas. Online platforms and open educational resources can provide students with personalized teaching and learning experiences. Artificial intelligence and virtual reality can make learning more engaging and relevant for the modern workforce. To make this vision a reality, investments in digital infrastructure and teacher training will be essential, ensuring every child has access to the education they deserve. Innovating to zero in education means creating lifelong learning opportunities for all, fostering skills that meet the evolving demands of the twenty-first century.

Zero Gender Inequality

Gender inequality remains a deep-seated challenge, impeding progress on multiple fronts. Women, despite constituting half the global population, continue to earn 23 per cent less than men on average.[22] They also perform three times more unpaid domestic work, which limits their economic opportunities. Gender-based violence, underrepresentation in leadership and systemic biases exacerbate these disparities. The COVID-19 pandemic further worsened these issues, placing an even heavier burden on women as care responsibilities surged, alongside a spike in gender-based violence.

To innovate towards zero gender inequality, we will need to address the core systemic barriers. Investments in education, skills development and equal employment opportunities will be crucial for empowering women. Companies will need to enforce equal pay for equal work and create inclusive environments where women can thrive. Expanding digital access for women will be another key lever, allowing them to engage in the economy more actively. By adopting policies that recognize unpaid care work and encourage shared household responsibilities, gender equality can become a reality. Innovating to zero means creating a world where women have equal opportunities, protection from violence and representation at all levels of society.

The larger picture here relates to zero discrimination, where discrimination based on race, gender, ethnicity, religion or other factors is eliminated. Innovations could include awareness initiatives, education, diversity and inclusion training programmes, and policy interventions that promote equality and respect for all individuals. This could be, on the one hand, rooting out inherent biases in society or laws and, on the other hand, empowering less-privileged communities by providing them with better opportunities and representation.

Zero Water Insecurity

Water insecurity remains a pressing global challenge, with over 2.2 billion people lacking access to safe drinking water and 3.5 billion without adequate sanitation. Climate change, pollution and growing populations are intensifying the issue, especially in vulnerable regions. Water-related diseases and insufficient sanitation pose severe public health risks, particularly in rural and developing areas. Despite water being a basic human right, billions still lack access to clean water and proper sanitation.

Today, water shortages affect almost 40 per cent of the world's population. Much of the global water crisis is manmade—a result of poor water management, wasteful consumption and outdated infrastructure. Cities like Cape Town, São Paulo, Jakarta and India's Silicon Valley, Bengaluru, are now facing severe water shortages, highlighting how urban populations are increasingly at risk. In some areas, clauses ensuring water availability are even being added to property agreements, underscoring how critical the issue has become.

Achieving zero water insecurity will require investing in sustainable water management, supporting infrastructure and conservation technologies. Innovating to zero in the context of water means scaling up technologies like rainwater harvesting, desalination and wastewater recycling—solutions that can alleviate the strain on freshwater resources. With a view to conserving water, reducing losses and delivering it efficiently, zero water waste will look to smart water-management systems that employ sensors, metres and predictive analytics to monitor usage, detect leaks and optimize distribution networks. In areas facing severe water stress, empowering local communities to manage their water systems will be essential. We've already seen how low-cost water filtration systems have revolutionized rural areas, providing clean drinking water on a large scale. The goal is to make these innovations universally accessible so that every person, no matter where they live, has reliable access to clean water and sanitation facilities.

Investments in sustainable water management, prioritization of sanitation infrastructure and community empowerment in managing their water resources responsibly will be vital. In addition, achieving zero water insecurity will require a cultural and behavioural reset towards more mindful water use, coupled with cutting-edge solutions to ensure equitable access for all.

Zero Energy Inequity

Despite progress, 675 million people still lack access to electricity, with energy demands increasing rapidly. The energy sector is the largest contributor to global greenhouse gas emissions, accounting for 60 per cent of the total.[23] With growing energy needs, particularly in developing regions, the focus must shift towards sustainable energy solutions to meet global targets while addressing climate change. Energy access remains unequal, with millions still living without electricity while the power demand grows. Fossil fuels continue to dominate energy production, contributing to climate change.

To innovate towards zero energy inequity, we will need to prioritize renewable energy solutions such as solar, wind and geothermal power. These technologies can provide reliable, affordable energy. Investments in clean energy infrastructure and smart grids will help scale renewable energy and reduce carbon emissions. Incentivizing research and development in green technologies will drive innovation, making sustainable energy accessible to all. By reducing reliance on fossil fuels and promoting energy efficiency, zero-carbon energy systems that power a sustainable future will be achievable.

Zero Unemployment

Although global unemployment rates improved in 2022, informal work and underemployment remain major challenges. Women, young people, and other vulnerable groups face greater difficulty in securing decent work, contributing to income inequality and poverty. Informal work still dominates many economies, leaving millions without legal protections or fair wages. Quality job creation is essential for reducing income inequality and ensuring long-term economic stability.

To achieve zero unemployment, it will be crucial to foster inclusive economic growth through entrepreneurship, digital innovation and education. Supporting entrepreneurship and the digital economy will generate high-quality jobs while addressing unemployment gaps. For example, promoting small and medium enterprises (SMEs) and investing in job-training programmes for growing sectors will provide sustainable employment. Governments should invest in small businesses, promote labour protections and support training programmes for emerging industries. By embracing advanced technologies, improving access to finance and leveraging smart policies, we will be able to create a labour market where decent work is available to everyone, and economic growth is inclusive and sustainable.

Zero Barriers to Industry

The global manufacturing sector has faced setbacks due to the pandemic and geopolitical roil, and recovery has been uneven. Access to mobile broadband is nearly universal, with 95 per cent of the global population now within reach of a network. However, many regions remain underserved, limiting their participation in the digital economy.

Achieving zero barriers to industry requires investing in resilient infrastructure, sustainable industrialization and fostering innovation, particularly in underserved regions. Robust transport, energy and communication networks are the backbone of industrial growth. Technologies like 5G, AI and the Internet of Things (IoT) can revolutionize industrial operations, driving both economic and environmental benefits. Strategic investments in green infrastructure and advanced technologies will enable less-developed regions to boost their manufacturing output, accelerating progress towards a more inclusive industrial future. By innovating to zero carbon emissions in industrial processes and expanding digital access, we can promote sustainable industrialization that benefits all.

Zero Inequality

Rising inequality, both within and between countries, poses a significant threat to long-term social and economic progress. The pandemic widened gaps in global income distribution. For the first time in three decades, between-country inequality surged due to the economic impacts of the pandemic. Social and economic disparities continue to erode people's sense of worth and security, and marginalized groups remain disproportionately affected.

Innovating to zero in this context means implementing policies that address inequality at its root. Social protection systems, investments in education and healthcare, and fair trade agreements will be crucial in levelling the playing field. For example, empowering marginalized communities through digital literacy programmes can enable them to access better job opportunities. For instance, project after project shows how underprivileged women in rural areas, after learning basic digital skills, start online businesses, dramatically improving their livelihoods. By leveraging innovation and technology, countries can reduce inequalities, ensure fair representation and promote inclusive growth. To innovate to zero here, global cooperation will be essential in fostering fair financial systems and reducing disparities within and between countries.

Zero Urban Inequality

Urbanization is accelerating at an unprecedented rate, with half of the world's population now living in cities—a figure projected to rise to 70 per cent by 2050. The rapid growth of cities, particularly in the developing world, has led to a significant worsening of urban inequality—an estimated 1.1 billion people currently live in slum-like conditions, lacking basic services such as sanitation and clean water. With an additional 2 billion people expected to live in cities over the next thirty years, urban planning has struggled to keep pace.

Innovating to zero in urban development involves redesigning cities to be more inclusive, safe, resilient and sustainable. Public transportation, affordable housing and green infrastructure will need to be prioritized. In my own experience, seeing the transformation of my neighbourhood from a chaotic, congested area into a pedestrian-friendly area with green spaces shows how effective urban planning can drastically improve quality of life. To achieve truly sustainable cities, we will need to focus on slum upgrades, invest in smart technologies for waste management and transportation, and ensure inclusive urban governance. Innovating to zero in this context means transforming cities into thriving, eco-friendly spaces where all residents have access to essential services and opportunities.

Zero Homelessness

Homelessness is a global issue that cuts across genders, age groups and ethnicities, located as it is at the 'intersection of public health, housing affordability, domestic violence, mental illness, substance misuse, urbanization, racial and gender discrimination, infrastructure, and unemployment'.[24] The United Nations Human Settlements Program estimates that 1.6 billion people live in poor housing conditions, with around 100 million people lacking housing entirely. Resolving this complex issue that affects individuals, communities and countries requires an innovating-to-zero approach that blends policy change, targeted interventions, community initiatives, housing reform and technological tools. Collective efforts by public and private organizations, reinforced by strong community commitment, will help in the push to zero homelessness.

Zero Traffic Congestion

Traffic congestion is a universal struggle, costing commuters precious time and reducing productivity. According to the 2023

TomTom Traffic Index, which analysed 387 cities across 55 countries, London—where I live—tops the list for the slowest average speed and worst congestion. A 6-mile trip now takes an extra minute compared to 2022. Many of the most congested cities are major economic hubs, with large populations and heavy commuter traffic. Other heavily impacted cities include Lima, Dublin, Milan, Bucharest, Brussels, Toronto, Pune, Bengaluru and Manila.[25] Unfortunately, wherever you go, traffic seems inescapable. It's a reminder of how urbanization continues to outpace infrastructure, leaving us stuck in gridlock as cities worldwide struggle to keep up.

So if there's one zero I would very much like to see, it would be zero traffic congestion. On the one hand, this could mean intelligent transportation systems that use traffic signal and route optimization algorithms or dynamic toll pricing to alleviate congestion, minimize emissions and streamline traffic flows. On the other hand, it could mean integrated multimodal transportation networks that would wean people off individual car use and support public transit use along with environment-friendly modes of transport like walking and cycling.

Zero Traffic Deaths

According to the WHO, road accidents result in a staggering 1.19 million fatalities every year and are the leading cause of death among children and young adults aged 5–29 years.[26] There's more bad news: vulnerable road users, including pedestrians, cyclists and motorcyclists account for more than half of all road traffic deaths. Apart from the unacceptable loss of human life, road traffic accidents cost countries an estimated 3 per cent of their GDP. Little surprise then that road-traffic fatalities and serious injuries need to be brought down to zero. This ideal would require targeted traffic planning that accommodates and prioritizes the safety of vulnerable road users, urban planning that looks at road redesign, greater public-awareness initiatives, the use of autonomous vehicles and, overarching all this, the collaboration between car manufacturers, technology developers, policymakers, urban planners to enhance driver, vehicle and road safety. This could add up to safer roads with zero traffic deaths for all road users.

Zero Waste

UNEP's *Global Waste Management Outlook 2024* predicts municipal solid waste–generation to reach 3.8 billion tons per year by 2050.[27] Mismanaged waste is a major contributor to rising GHG emissions, environmental degradation and adverse health impacts, especially in lower-income communities and developing nations. These effects often disproportionately affect vulnerable populations, including women and children. The idea of zero waste aims, if not to eliminate then, at any rate, to minimize waste generation and maximize resource efficiencies through intelligent waste-management practices.[28]

The current rate of consumption and production is unsustainable, with natural resources being depleted faster than the planet can replenish them. If global trends continue, by 2050 the planet will need the equivalent of nearly three Earths to provide sufficient natural resources. In 2021, fossil fuel subsidies soared to $732 billion, nearly double the amount spent in 2020, hindering efforts to transition to clean energy. Meanwhile, food waste continues to be a major issue—13.2 per cent of the world's food is lost post-harvest, even as 828 million people face hunger.

This involves a range of strategies—from repairing, reusing and recycling materials to designing products with minimal packaging and waste in mind. Circular-economy principles offer a roadmap for achieving complete recyclability, where products are managed cradle-to-cradle, reducing waste at every stage of their lifecycle.

Zero waste management will also call for community-backed waste-management campaigns, encouraging businesses to integrate sustainability into their business models, and reducing food waste to help lower the environmental footprint of production.

It will mean adopting advanced technologies like AI, automation and robotics to streamline processes. AI-driven waste-management solutions, including sensor-based bins, can optimize sorting and recycling while reducing human error. Telematics, electrification and autonomous trucks will enhance the productivity, safety and reliability of waste-management operations. Additionally, waste-to-energy facilities can transform organic waste into renewable energy, feeding power back into the system and supporting sustainable waste operations.

Ultimately, zero waste will be about rethinking the entire lifecycle of waste, transforming it into a system where resources are continually cycled back into production, resulting in a truly sustainable, circular economy. In this vision, waste will become a thing of the past: we will be able to ensure that the cycle of consumption and production works in harmony with the planet's natural limits, and that future consumption patterns do not exceed the Earth's capacity to regenerate its resources. If businesses and consumers worldwide embrace mindful consumption and production practices, we stand every chance of achieving zero waste and creating a more responsible and sustainable production ecosystem.

Zero Emissions

Climate change is the most pressing global challenge, with rising emissions driving unpredictable weather patterns, sea-level rise, and increasingly severe weather events, all of which disproportionately affect vulnerable communities. Between 2010 and 2020, regions with high vulnerability saw mortality rates from floods, droughts and storms that were fifteen times higher than regions with lower vulnerability. Sea levels reached record highs in 2022, contributing to the displacement of millions and exacerbating global migration challenges. Without urgent intervention, climate change could undo decades of progress and fuel further instability.

Innovating to zero in this context will mean climate-change resilience and mitigation. It will call for affordable, scalable solutions that can mitigate climate-change impacts while transitioning to a low-carbon economy. Strengthening resilience to climate-related disasters through better infrastructure, early warning systems and adaptive planning will help safeguard vulnerable populations. We have repeatedly seen how green energy projects reduce carbon emissions while providing jobs in the regions in which they are set up, underlining how low-carbon solutions can also drive economic growth. By investing in renewable energy, enhancing climate resilience and coordinating global efforts, we will have the ability to halt emissions and protect ecosystems for future generations.

Zero Marine Pollution

Oceans cover over 70 per cent of the Earth's surface and are critical to life on Earth, but pollution, overfishing and climate change threaten marine ecosystems. Innovating to zero marine pollution involves addressing ocean acidification, reducing plastic waste and promoting sustainable fishing. By 2040, ocean plastic pollution is expected to double or triple, building on the 17 million metric tons already present as of 2021. Ocean acidification, caused by the absorption of CO_2, has made ocean waters 30 per cent more acidic since pre-industrial times. This change endangers marine life, disrupts the food web and undermines the livelihoods of billions who depend on the ocean for food and resources.

To innovate to zero, we will need to reverse the trend of ocean degradation by investing in marine conservation, improving waste management and regulating harmful fishing practices. For instance, countries can collaborate to reduce ocean acidification by lowering global carbon emissions and promoting sustainable fishing. By supporting scientific research, enhancing conservation efforts and adopting sustainable practices, we will be on course to restore ocean health.

Zero Deforestation

Forests are vital for biodiversity and carbon sequestration, yet deforestation and land degradation continue at alarming rates. Terrestrial ecosystems, which include forests, grasslands and wetlands, are essential for sustaining human life. Forests, in particular, provide livelihoods, contribute to biodiversity, and play a crucial role in absorbing CO_2. However, forest coverage has been declining, dropping from 31.9 per cent in 2000 to 31.2 per cent in 2020, driven largely by deforestation and land degradation. Over 100 million hectares of productive land were degraded annually between 2015 and 2019, affecting the well-being of 1.3 billion people. Biodiversity is also under threat, with 21 per cent of reptile species classified as endangered in 2022.

Innovating to zero deforestation will mean adopting sustainable land-management practices and scaling reforestation efforts. By promoting biodiversity conservation, restoring degraded land and implementing policies to halt habitat destruction, we will be able to protect terrestrial ecosystems. Governments, businesses and communities must adopt sustainable land-management practices, including reforestation and afforestation projects to protect ecosystems, reduce carbon footprints and prevent biodiversity loss. Innovating to zero here will mean ensuring that human development no longer comes at the cost of the planet's natural heritage.

Zero Violence

Conflict, violence and weak institutions undermine social and economic development. Between 2021 and 2022, civilian deaths from the world's deadliest conflicts increased by 53 per cent. Violence, insecurity and corruption not only destroy lives but also erode trust in institutions and hinder economic growth. The forced displacement of 108.4 million people by the end of 2022 further demonstrates the global scale of these issues.[29]

Innovating to zero violence could mean identifying strategies to root out violence in all its myriad forms, whether gun violence, bullying or gender-based violence. By promoting accountable governance, respect for the rule of law, ensuring access to justice and building strong, transparent institutions, we will be able to create societies where individuals feel safe and empowered. It's a complex and arduous undertaking no doubt, one that would require concerted, collective, community-led action to build the foundations of a zero-violence society based on equity, inclusion, peace and cooperation.

Allied with this would be the idea of a zero crime rate. After all, who wouldn't want to live with a sense of enhanced public safety and security?[30] We could be looking at smart cities that turn to data analytics, predictive algorithms, surveillance technologies and real-time crime mapping. Add to this smart street lighting to deter anti-social activity, greater community involvement and zero tolerance policing … and the result could be zero crime rates. Would that mean the need for zero police?

Zero Inequity in Global Partnerships

Achieving sustainable development requires global cooperation and equitable partnerships. Innovating to zero in global partnerships will mean mobilizing resources and fostering collaboration between individuals and institutions, governments and civil society, public and private players, consumers and commercial entities. This is how every stakeholder in the global ecosystem is recognized and embraced in the quest to realize vision zero. This means building trust, sharing resources and working collectively to achieve shared objectives.

Conclusion

The vision of innovating to zero is both ambitious and transformative, aiming to eliminate some of humanity's most pressing challenges—hunger, poverty, violence, inequality and environmental degradation. It offers a powerful framework to reimagine societies, economies and cultures by fostering partnerships that promote peace, justice and inclusivity. Through this lens, we can build effective institutions that protect ecosystems and promote sustainable use of our planet's resources. This vision calls for the transformation of urban spaces to be resilient and inclusive, while also safeguarding our land, air and water. Anchored in climate resilience and mitigation, innovating to zero seeks urgent action against climate change, driving sustainable consumption and production patterns that aim to reduce inequality and foster a fair, inclusive global community.

This ambitious concept extends beyond mere survival; it envisions thriving societies with clean energy, secure water systems and resilient infrastructure. It targets not only economic growth but sustainable growth that provides decent work for all, promotes gender equality and ensures lifelong learning for everyone. It seeks universal access to health, revolutionized agriculture to end hunger and financial inclusion that lifts people out of poverty. Such a vision, though ideal, is not an overnight transformation. The journey will be long and hard, requiring sustained effort, innovation and collaboration.

But even as we begin, every step we take towards this ideal world is a victory in itself. The progress we make, no matter how incremental, has the potential to fundamentally reshape our world for the better. Innovating to zero is more than just a destination—it is a guiding philosophy that will, with time, lead to a more just, sustainable and equitable future for all. While the path may be arduous, the rewards along the way will be extraordinary.

10

HOW TO BUILD A ZERO-VISION STRATEGY

In previous chapters, we have learnt about the power of zero and how it can manifest in multiple ways across businesses, societies and our personal lives. In this chapter, we will explore how to design, develop, implement and deliver a zero-vision strategy. My examples focus on the corporate world but are equally applicable to any organization, from NGOs to policymaking institutes.

Examples from the corporate world are innumerable: from German automotive parts manufacturer Continental, whose zero vision encompasses zero fatalities, zero injuries, zero crashes, to Danish beer-maker Carlsberg, whose 'Together Towards Zero Program' seeks to eliminate zero water waste; from US automaker GM's Factory Zero, its first assembly plant focused entirely on EV production, to Tesla's Zero Emissions vehicles; from Diet Coke to Pepsi Black, it is all about vision zero. And then there are other interpretations of vision zero: Indian FMCG Britannia's Nutrition Foundation that strives towards zero malnutrition, NGOs like Save the Children whose vision zero targets the end of poverty and hunger, government-backed policies like the UK's Net Zero Carbon Emissions by 2050, the City of Los Angeles' commitment to reach zero traffic deaths, Singapore's zero-tolerance policy on drugs, and the EU's zero vision on occupational safety that addresses work-related fatalities, accidents and ill health.

And there you have it: multiple approaches, interpretations and motivations for zero vision. And while these might vary, I believe that the fundamental building blocks for a zero-vision strategy are broadly the same. In this chapter, I will share my very own version of a ten-step change process that will, hopefully, help you successfully ideate and implement a zero vision.

Building a Zero-Vision Strategy

Step 1: Start with an environment scan, assess the mega trends that are shaping the world

I am a firm believer—and, somewhat biased I must admit—in the defining impact of mega trends. My bias can be attributed to my being a foresighting expert. That said, I think you will agree with me when I say that any sound strategy needs to start with a careful look ahead at the future, the mega trends that will shape it, and an understanding about how our future world might evolve. At MarketsandMarkets, we have identified twelve mega trends that will shape our future world (Chart 10.1).

In turn, these mega trends comprise key sub-trends and enablers (Chart 10.2) that are split by horizons.

This trend wheel developed by MarketsandMarkets evaluates mega trends in terms of certainty and time horizon: Horizon 1 are the 'knowns', that is, trends/enablers that are here and now, Horizon 2 are the 'somewhat knowns', and Horizon 3 are trends that are further afield and riddled with 'unknowns'.

My article in *Forbes* examines these trends in more detail[1] and, if you want to deep-dive even further, you can always check out

CHART 10.1 : TOP 12 MEGA TRENDS IMPACTING OUR GLOBAL WORLD

Definition : Disruptive trends are high impact **global happenings** that impact the future world with their far- reaching spread on business, societies, economies, cultures and citizen lives.

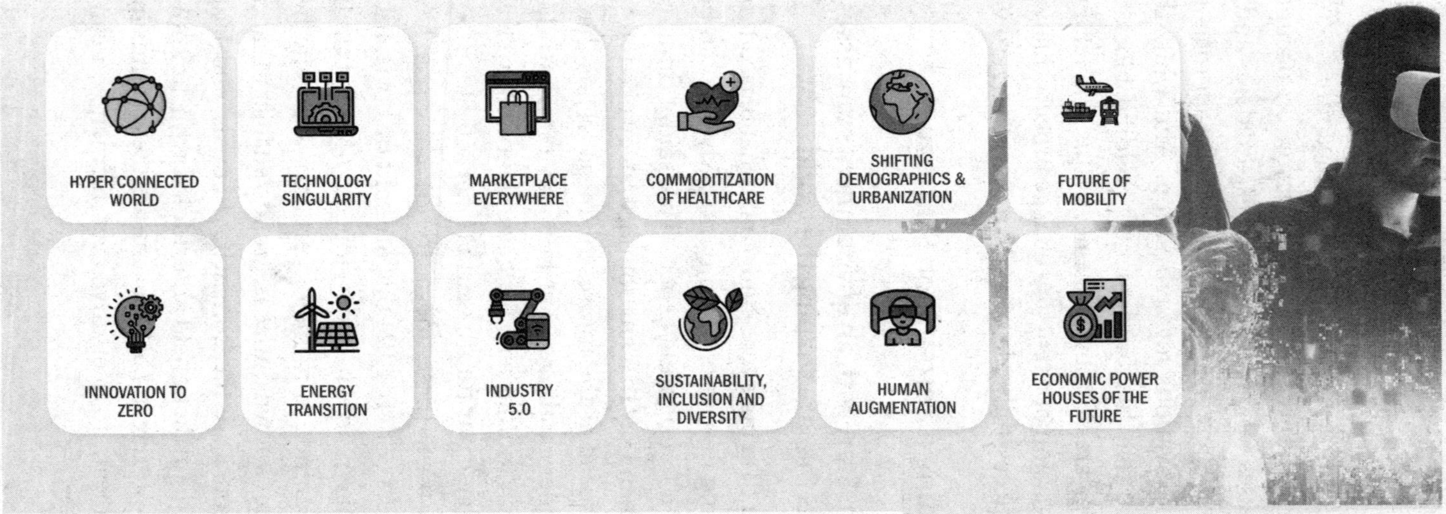

Source : Markets and Markets

CHART 10.2:TRENDS WHEEL

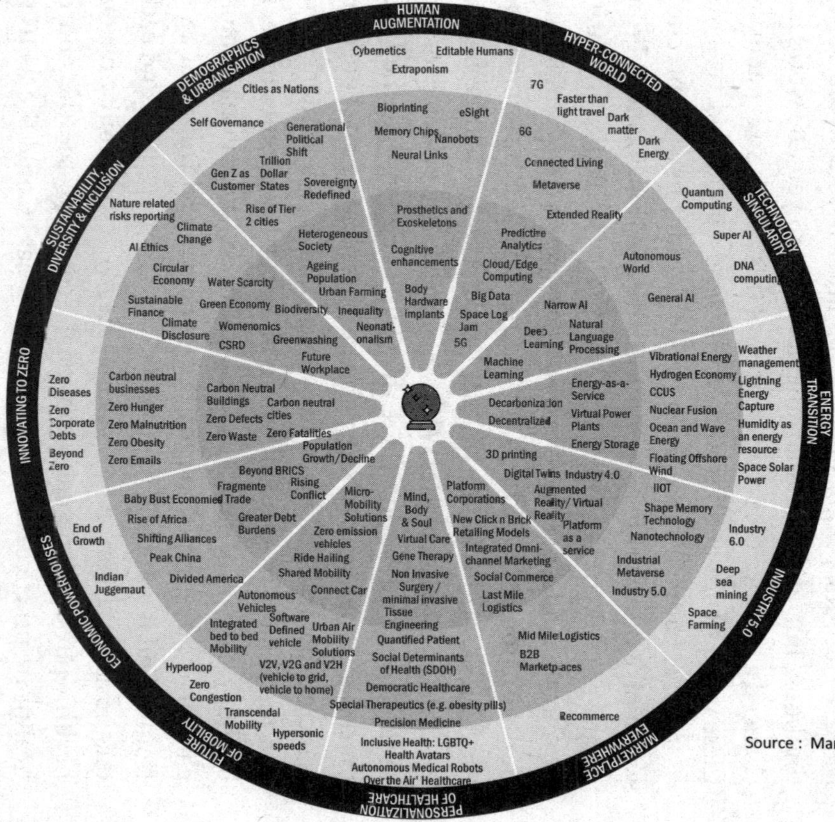

- HORIZON 1: THE KNOWN
- HORIZON 2: THE SOMEWHAT KNOWN
- HORIZON 3: THE UNKNOWN

Source : Markets and Markets

CSRD : Corporate Sustainability Reporting Directive

MarketsandMarket's Foresighting service.[2] Then there's also *New Mega Trends: Implications for Our Future Lives*, the precursor to this book. But, and I would be the first to warn you, the world has changed a lot since then. Annexure 2 of this book also expands on these mega trends and I would recommend a good read.

At what pace will these mega trends play out? In what direction will it take our world? How will our lives be transformed? From what I see, a hyper-connected world and technology-singularity (artificial intelligence) are the two biggest mega trends impacting our world today. However, if you ask me what the most *important* mega trend of the future will be, I predict that it will be health, wellness and wellbeing (HWW). We already see evidence of this in the developed world, where the GDP of nations like the US is touching 20 per cent, where populations are aging and longevity is increasing. Indeed, one in five of us will live to be centenarians, and the person(s) who will live to blow out 150 candles on their birthday cakes has/have already been born. We will have more chronic diseases and healthcare's business model will pivot away from a 'find it and fix it' approach towards a prevention and early diagnosis paradigm. As we assume greater responsibility for our health—physical, mental, emotional—could we see the end of healthcare practices as we know them today? Could the focus of healthcare shift further away from primary care towards more secondary and tertiary care? Could new medical technologies like gene editing, advanced gene and cell therapies and tissue engineering revolutionize the way healthcare is envisioned and delivered? From another perspective, how will a focus on inclusivity in terms of recognizing social determinants of health (SDOH), more democratized and accessible health, and the embrace of specific cohorts like LGBTQI affect our engagement with health? How will autonomous medical robots, special therapeutics and new AI-aided medical interventions impact healthcare delivery? How will personalized treatment regimes and targeted drug development link to improved patient outcomes?

Trends like HWW will manifest in anything and everything we do. For example, healthcare + mobility will integrate as we already see in the ubiquitous smart-watch phenomenon. Today, smart watches are not merely fashion statements or devices that tell time: they are, more importantly, omnipresent healthcare collaborators. After all, they track and support your fitness levels, monitor your heart rate, note how many calories you have burnt (never enough in my case), keep 'watch' over your oxygen levels, alert you to erratic sleep patterns, observe your blood pressure and encourage you to increase your physical movements. From Apple Watches and Fitbits to the Oura Ring that I gave my wife as a Christmas present (well worth the $500+ investment), HWW is a daily constant in our lives. Add to this, smart weighing scales that go beyond merely warning you of creeping weight gain to measuring BMI, body-fat percentage and muscle mass, to offering many other wellness features.

As you will notice in Chart 10.2, there are only a clutch of sub-trends in the outer Horizon 3. But these are extremely disruptive. Trends like quantum computing, hypersonic speeds for travel, dark energy, deepsea mining, end of growth, and many others in the outer rings of 'unknowns', are game changers that suggest a very different world in the 2050s to the world we live in now. We can think more deeply about these at another time. For the present, all we need to be is mindful that the trends in Horizon 2 and 3 will deeply influence how we define and measure zero in the future.

Of course, it is not just enough to have an understanding of these mega trends, it is as important to identify and define the macro factors that impact your industry and your business. And for this, it is important to define your 'business'. What do I mean by that? Well, my spiel to car companies in the automotive industry is that you are not so much in the business of making cars as you are in the business of enabling mobility. This means understanding how people move from A to B which, in turn, has an impact on how, which, where and when a car is used. Likewise, companies in the beverage industry that are in the business of making fizzy drinks need to understand changing consumption habits and trends, such as HWW, in order to identify the opportunities in and challenges to their industry.

Chart 10.3 shows the macro factors that impact the auto industry and how the industry uses them to achieve differentiation. Similarly, such macro factors should be developed for your industry based on the mega trends and trend wheel shown in charts 10.1 and 10.2.

These macro factors change over time and an understanding of that shift is important. For example, in the 1990s, BMW talked itself up as 'the ultimate driving machine' since factors like driving pleasure were key macro factors for differentiation at that time. Things changed in the 2000s, reflective of a time when sustainability and the environment had become important factors of differentiation. During the noughties, therefore, BMW relabeled itself as a brand noted for 'Efficient Dynamics'. Now, when you read deeper into BMW's messaging, this is what stood out: it held onto its brand image of being a vehicle for piston heads (like me) who valued a good speedy and curvy drive, *and* for people (like me) who were also becoming increasingly environment conscious. The German automaker cleverly adopted this messaging, while continuing to churn out top-rate vehicles and the equally top-rate inbuilt technologies that powered them. In short, BMW recognized the winds of (mega trend) change and led the way with their, by now iconic, Brand i. Their

CHART 10.3 : MACRO FACTORS IMPACTING THE AUTO INDUSTRY

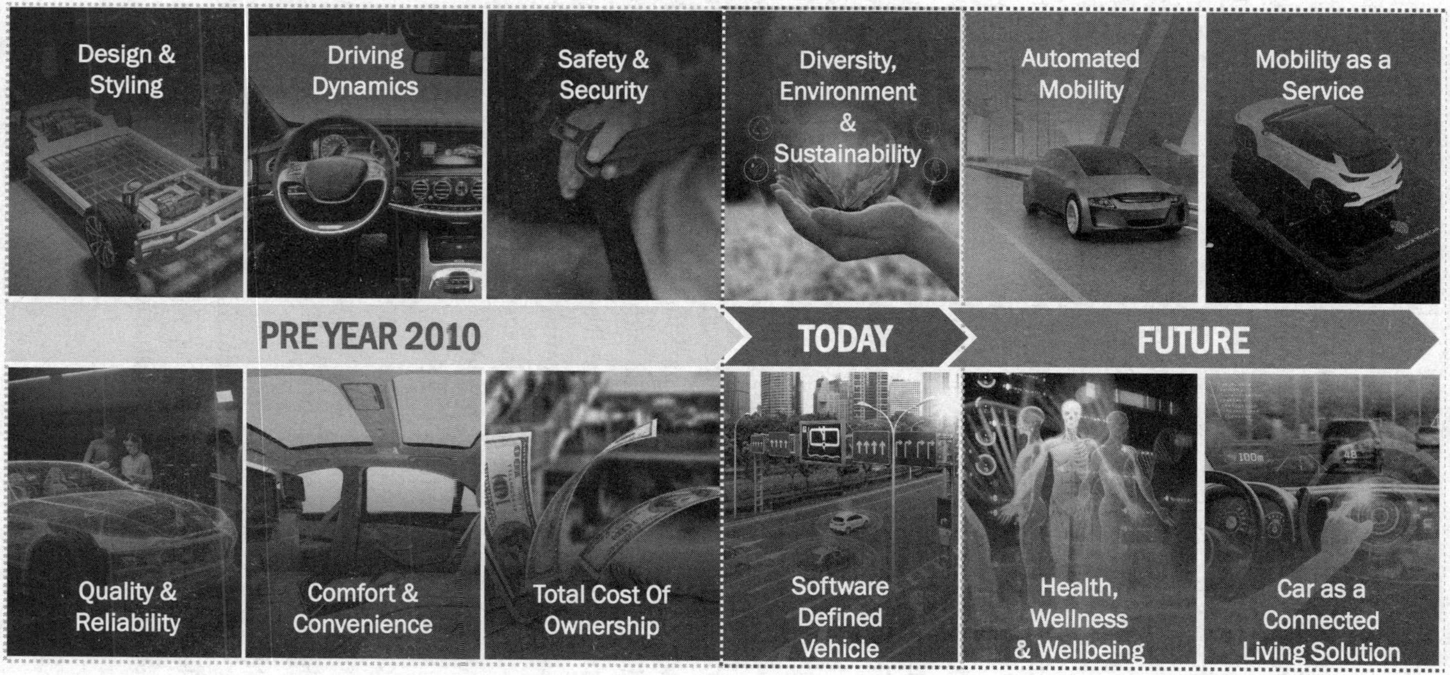

trailblazing i3 and i8—gosh, how desperately I wanted an i8 when it was launched—electric-car family was at the forefront of zero-emissions innovation well before a certain Elon Musk entered the fray with Tesla.

So, if we examine these macro factors and the direction in which they are developing, we can see that health, wellness and wellbeing, connected living, autonomous world, and environmental sustainability will be key themes in the future.

Take autonomous world, for example. The SAE defines it in Levels 1 to 5, with Level 5 being completely autonomous vehicles that would drive from Boston to Washington without the need for any driving intervention from you. What functionalities do Levels 1-5 correspond with? According to the SAE, Level 1 autonomy begins with feet off (for example, cruise control), followed by hands off (steering wheel assist as we see in premium Teslas), eyes off (traffic-jam assist features), mind off (features like low-speed automation, hands-off parking) and, eventually, to brain off in Level 5. Just imagine a car without a steering wheel or brakes. Not to worry though, we are still a good decade or more away before we reach complete autonomy.

So, my thinking on these macro factors leads me to believe that car companies should be looking to develop vehicles which combine mobility + health, wellness and wellbeing + zero emissions + connected + autonomous vehicle features. In other words, an industry that brings out zero emission cars + zero latency + zero mind/brains (level 4 and 5) + zero stress (or zero congestion).

To summarize, an understanding of mega trends and macro factors will help determine which zero-vision strategy will best suit your industry and customers' unmet needs.

Step 2: Set the vision, align it to your organization's mission and values

Corporates have a defined product conceptualization process and this process can be tweaked to develop a zero-vision strategy. To give you a sense of what I mean, let me explain a process with which I am familiar—the product-development cycle of the auto industry.

Most vehicle manufacturers identify and definc the macro factors and mega trends according to which they will develop their products. For example, in the early 2000s, Volvo focused on seven factors (Chart 10.4), Ford (Chart 10.5) used the DCDQ philosophy (also called the Ford DNA) and BMW (Chart 10.6) used a pyramid which clearly distinguished special differentiation attributes from more standard ones.

Chart 10.5 shows Ford's DCDQ brand values—as expressed internally within Ford and defined as dependable, contemporary, driving quality. These values are embraced across design, engineering and marketing before the product is, ultimately, released into the consumer world.

Vehicle manufacturers typically use this philosophy when it comes to develop their next generation products and achieve product differentiation. A case in point is Volvo and its XC90 which was the first SUV that it launched in 2002.

If you are of my vintage, you might remember that almost a quarter century ago in 2000, Ford Explorers were beset by incidents of rollovers, resulting in about 200 deaths and 700 injuries in the US.[3] In many cases, defective tires, particularly tire separation, were found to be a contributing factor in the mishaps. Similarly, around the same time, the Mercedes A Class also suffered from a rash of vehicle rollovers. In this case, however, tires played a subordinate role. The main issue was a combination

CHART 10.4 : PRODUCT CONCEPTUALIZATION PROCESS - VOLVO CASE STUDY

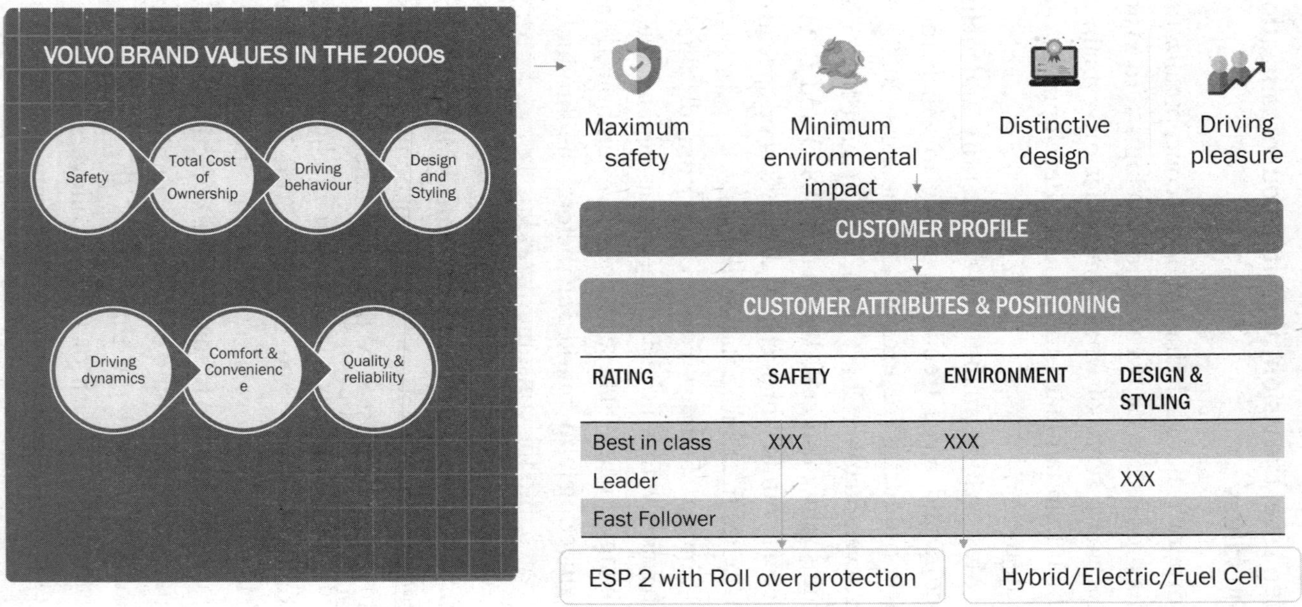

CHART 10.5 : FORD DCDQ

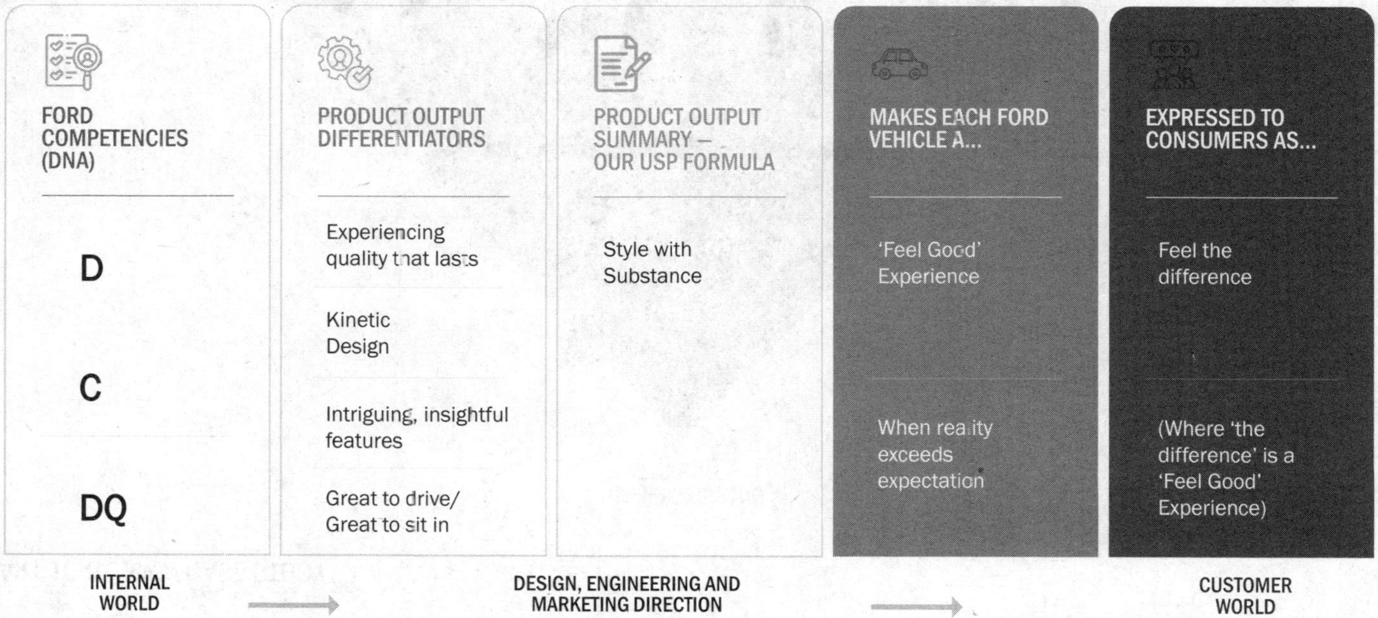

Source: Boston Consulting Group

CHART 10.6 : BMW CASE STUDY

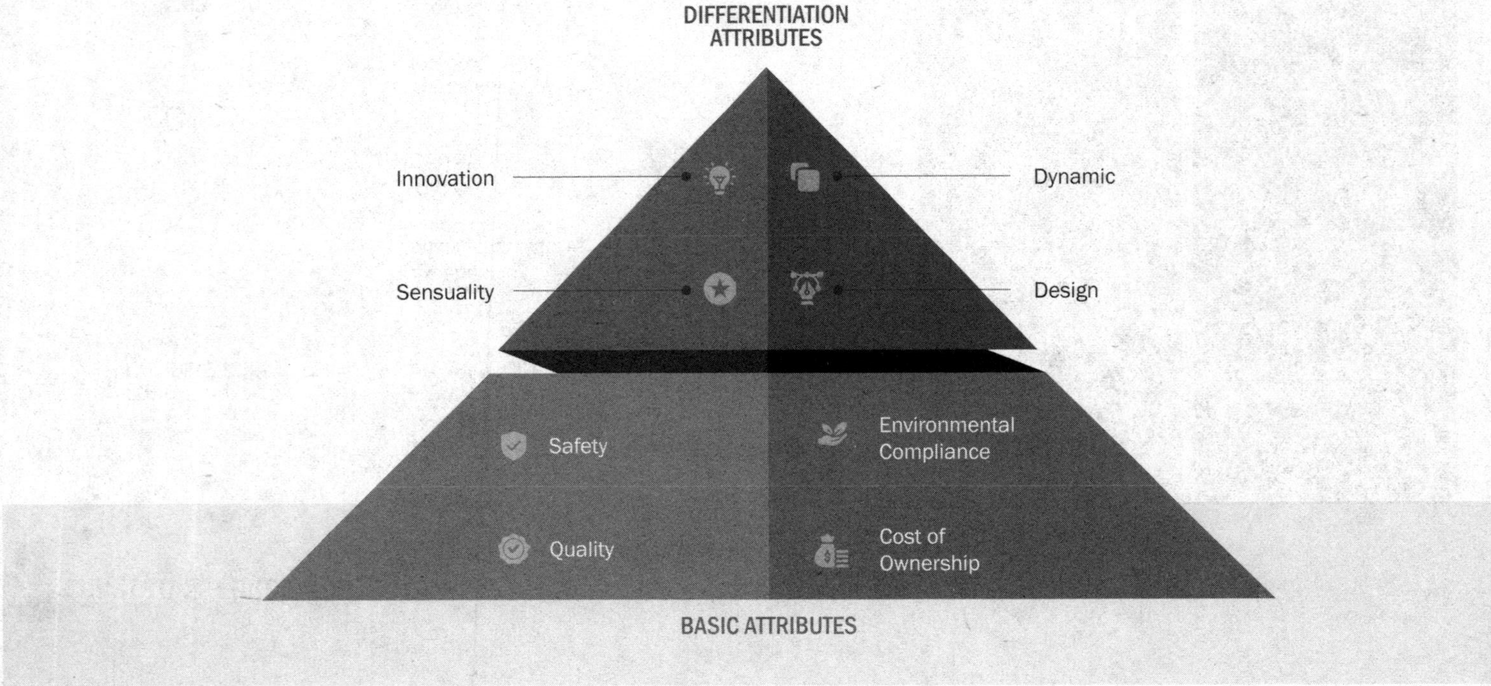

of the position of the centre of gravity and the chassis position in an intense driving situation. This was a time when SUVs were starting to get popular and people were swapping out their saloons and hatchbacks for SUVs.

The story isn't over. As Ford and Mercedes worked on damage control, Volvo was swinging into action. As part of its product conceptualization process (Chart 10.4), it defined four key factors to achieve differentiation—maximum safety, minimum environmental impact, distinctive design and driving pleasure. Typically, in terms of these categories, vehicle manufacturers decide where they want to be 'best-in-class', where 'leaders' and where they will aim to be, the rather euphemistically termed 'fast followers' (the more truthful term, I think, would be 'snoozers losers'). Volvo based its brand positioning to always be 'best-in-class' in terms of safety. The frequency of SUVs toppling over at high speeds spurred its mission of becoming the first car company to offer customers an SUV with zero rollover. Their engineering teams were, accordingly, tasked with finding a technology solution that would enable this. It was fortuitous timing since this period coincided with the launch of the first electronic stability control (ESC) system.

ESC, also referred to as dynamic stability control (DSC) or electronic stability programme (ESP), improves a vehicle's stability by detecting and reducing loss of traction (skidding). Wheel sensors detect the beginning of a slide and apply the appropriate amount of braking pressure to individual wheels to regain stability. Braking is automatically applied to wheels individually, such as the outer front wheel to counter oversteer, or the inner rear wheel to counter understeer. ESC systems also reduce engine power until control is regained. These systems were introduced in the late 1990s and made standard in vehicles around 2011–14.

Volvo engineers, therefore, decided to add roll stability control to the ESP solution on the XC90. This meant that Volvo was then able to market it as the safest car with zero rollover and reaffirm its position as the vehicle manufacturer with the safest car. It is no mean feat that the XC90 is often referred to as the safest car in the world with no driver or passenger fatalities having been reported on this model in the UK since 2004.

Carrying forward its claim to being the vehicle manufacturer with the best-in-class safety record, Volvo laid down its ambitious Vision 2020 of zero deaths. It intended to achieve this through a raft of active and passive safety features in its cars. It didn't quite succeed although, to be fair, much of the blame was assigned to alcohol-impaired drivers rather than the cars themselves. What is undeniable is that Volvo has produced some of the world's safety vehicles. Over time, it has dealt with the menace of drunk driving by incorporating alcohol locks and driver drowsiness systems in its cars.

Today, zero accidents is a fundamental mantra of Volvo and the company asserts that no one has died in a Volvo in the last two years.

The young grandson of the Volvo XC90 is the new Volvo EX90 launched in 2023. It is fully electric, has zero emissions and comes with an advanced zero accidents safety system—the 'zero-collisions visions system'—which includes advanced sensing technologies powered by lidars, radars and cameras that detect potential risks that lie beyond the driver's line of sight. So the power of zero in Volvo and in cars continues.

Step 3: Identify unmet needs

Once you have accomplished steps 1 and 2, it is important you evaluate and identify unmet customer needs that can be resolved with a vision-zero strategy. As we read in the previous section, Volvo did just that with its XC90.

Another good example, and continuing with our automotive analogies, is BMW, which developed the i3 Zero Emission EV to address the demands of urban customers. It was meant to be a car for use in a mega city and was conceived in response to the mega trend of urbanization. BMW realized that it needed to look at the demands of its customers not just in mega cities but increasingly in mega regions as well. By then, mega regions had become a reality—cities that had expanded beyond their own borders to combine with neighboring satellite towns. Examples abound from JoToria (Johannesburg and Pretoria) in South Africa to the National Capital Region (NCR) in India which covers the Delhi metro region and neighbouring cities like Gurgaon, Noida and others to form a mega region housing over 34 million inhabitants. In short, BMW needed to develop a vehicle for customers living in these mega cities and mega regions. When they did their research, they found that one of the main challenges associated with driving in congested cities was the inability of cars to do two-point turns or park in congested spaces. This was a result of cars, on average, having a turning radius of 10.4–10.7 m. Interestingly, however, London's iconic black cabs could both execute flawless two point turns and squeeze into tight spaces as legislation demanded they have under 9 m turning radius. BMW understood this unmet customer need and consequently became the first vehicle manufacturer to develop a car (which was not a taxi) with the lowest turning radius.

Another example is Zara. As discussed in Chapter 2, the Spanish retail giant's invention of the concept of zero design-to-shelves response time was based on its understanding of customers' unmet need of aligning their fashion choices to dynamic factors like day-to-day weather or wanting to look like their celebrity idol. This isn't a case of passing customer fancy, it is serious business. Need I add more about this trend than a single word—Swiftonimics: the economic phenomena where global music star Taylor Swift's fashion choices have led to brands going viral and denim skorts, crochet corsets, cowboy boots and sparkly bodysuits flying off the shelves. So with customers' fashion demands changing almost daily, what does a clothing brand have to do to stay relevant? Zara realized that to stay competitive and à la mode, it needed a completely reimagined supply chain solution that would compress the time it took from identifying what was in vogue to stocking it on their shelves.

Most innovations or inventions are borne out of an understanding of customers' unmet needs and then designing a solution around it. The difference between developing a product that just about meets the customer's need to one that exceeds expectations and creates a zero-vision strategy depends on how far boundaries are pushed and the level of disruption you are willing to envision.

Thus, identifying unmet customer need leads to the next important step—Step 4—in setting a zero vision.

Step 4: Set the vision, be bold, be disruptive

> 'Let us think the unthinkable, let us do the undoable, let us prepare to grapple with the ineffable itself and see if we may not eff it after all.'
>
> —Douglas Adams

Wiser words were never said and this is exactly the attitude one needs when it comes to setting the zero vision.

Toyota was the first automaker to develop a hybrid vehicle. It was unique at the time, and it met the company's goal of strengthening its sustainability and environment credentials while addressing the unmet needs of customers looking for an environment-friendly vehicle. But, Toyota did not push hard enough or far enough. All of which meant it was not good enough to set a zero vision, and that is where Nissan stepped in to steal the crown.

We had earlier discussed how Volvo's product conceptualization process in Chart 10.4 cleaved around three degrees of positioning—best-in-class, leadership and fast follower. To this, we now need to add a fourth measure—disrupter.

In my experience, setting a zero vision requires you to be adventurous, disruptive and have the confidence to raise the bar high. You need to stretch your imagination to the point of lunacy and believe that it can be done. And that is exactly what Nissan did (Chart 10.7). It decided that it was not enough to develop just another hybrid vehicle to compete with Toyota. Instead, it ratcheted the bar several notches higher. Its seemingly crazy and implausible idea at the time was to develop a completely zero-emission vehicle, a vehicle that would emit no tailpipe emissions. In hindsight, what an insanely fabulous breakthrough given that by 2035, electric cars will outrun internal combustion engines.

There are innumerable examples of organizations that have been galvanized by such disruptive visions. They have abandoned their comfort zones and leaped into the great unknown. For them, it has not been about cautious incremental improvements, it has been about bold, almost unreal transformation. And that is exactly what is needed when it comes to setting the zero vision.

These are a few suggestions to consider when developing a zero vision. Some might be obvious, others not.

CHART 10.7 : NISSAN CASE STUDY

- Define the pain points of your industry. For example, cars release emissions and cause deaths. What if we had cars that had no emissions?
- Set quantifiable targets. For example, when Toyota and Honda created hybrid vehicles, there was a huge emphasis on reducing CO_2 emissions. In 2016, emission-reduction targets were set to below 120 gm CO_2/km.
- Throw yourself a challenge, bordering on lunacy or, as Elon Musk would say, embrace your 'insane mode'. Toyota pulled off a stunning coup, offering up hybrid vehicles that, at 60 gm CO_2/km, emitted half EU mandated carbon emissions targets of 120 gm CO_2/km. While this truly an achievement, how about pegging the bar even higher and saying we will develop a car that will emit zero emissions?
- And, finally, once you have a clear vision, look at what needs to be done to achieve it, whether from a product, technology or service perspective.

To reiterate, the important part in this step is to fearlessly push boundaries and think the unthinkable.

Step 5: Do a macro-to-micro analysis and define key attributes

Once you have set the vision, it is important to transform it into reality. To do so, I recommend undertaking a macro-to-micro analysis and defining the key attributes that will help shape the vision.

Let me illustrate my point. For instance, when Volvo says it wants to be the world leader in making zero accident vehicles, it needs to back this up with a detailed roadmap on how it plans to get to this goal.

In the auto industry, safety is defined as a function of active and passive safety.

Active safety systems are those that pre-empt an accident from occurring or, at any rate, actively help reduce its impact. Examples of such systems are anti-lock braking systems, electronic stability control systems, autonomous braking assist that apply brakes even when you as driver have not, lane departure or management systems, intelligent speed adaption, and many others.

Passive safety systems are systems that minimize, reduce and mitigate post-collision impact. The simplest form of a passive-safety system in cars is the seat belt. We also have air bags, child seats, head rests and, in modern cars, crumple zones and pedestrian-protection systems.

Logically then, for a company like Volvo to develop a zero-accidents vision, it needs to work on its active-safety systems strategy in order to avoid accidents before they can happen. However, if its vision is to realize zero accidents *and* zero fatalities, then it also needs to augment its cars with passive safety features that mitigate serious injury or deaths.

And so, it is crucial to recognize that in developing a zero vision, the vision needs to be broken down into its individual constituents so as to understand and tackle them at base level.

Step 6: Zero vision comes in pairs and groups, not in isolation and with a new business model

My involvement with zero vision has left me convinced that such a vision is best developed when working on a few of them together, rather than discretely, as they tend to complement and augment each other. Volvo's zero fatalities strategy has to cover both zero accidents *and* zero injuries *and* needs to be supported, as we see in its new Volvo EX90, with a zero-emission vehicle.

As we saw in the Nissan example when it set about developing a zero-emission vehicle, a key element of the strategy was to also develop a fully connected vehicle. Similarly, one of the reasons behind Tesla's success has been its all-embracing approach. While developing its zero emissions EVs, it completely upturned vehicle architecture as the automotive industry knew it, creating a fully connected vehicle platform that, from the outset, mirrored the mobile phone industry with the aim of enabling seamless, software over the air updates (SOTA). To this end, Tesla radically changed the vehicle's electric/electronic architecture, building in centralized electronic control units as opposed to what traditional car companies were doing—building isolated, decentralized electronic control units, an oversight that has come back to haunt old school automakers since it precludes the possibility of over the air updates like that of Tesla's.

New Business Models Enabling Zero Strategy

In my book *New Mega Trends*, I explored an intriguing parallel between warfare and business models. Just as the invention of a new weapon can tilt the scales in favour of one of the combatants, innovative and sustainable business models can give companies a competitive edge in an ever-evolving marketplace. In the same way that warfare has evolved through five generations—the linear formations of Napoleonic columns, the trench warfare and mass sieges of WWI and WWII, the blitzkrieg tactics of Nazi Germany with its surprise, lightning-fast, coordinated land, sea and air attacks, the guerrilla warfare that marked conflicts in Vietnam, Afghanistan and Iraq, and now cyber and urban warfare—business models have also undergone their own transformation. We have moved from the conventional models of the Industrial Revolution to convenience (think McDonald's), magnitude (hypermarkets and Walmart) to dot-com giants (eBay, Amazon, Netflix), and now, to the fifth generation with its convergence of Web 2.0 and app-based platforms.

In both warfare and business, technology, innovation and a certain boldness (or entrepreneurial spirit) play pivotal roles. However, while technological superiority is crucial, it doesn't guarantee success. The US' experiences in Vietnam, Afghanistan and Iraq illustrate this well; despite advanced military technology, they struggled to achieve their objectives. The same principle applies to business: even the most advanced technology won't ensure success unless backed by a solid product and smart positioning.

Throughout my career, I've helped clients develop new business models that harness technological shifts and trends. In recent years, my focus has been on moving from CAPEX to OPEX-based models, creating revenue opportunities across the product lifecycle, and even exploring outcome-based models. These approaches are especially relevant as we move towards a net zero future.

The Boston Consulting Group (BCG)[4] estimates that achieving net zero will require \$3 to \$5 trillion annually. In Asia alone, the market for corporate climate action could be worth over \$4 trillion by 2030, potentially creating up to 230 million jobs. This shift towards net zero, or zero vision, offers organizations an opportunity to innovate and build new business models that not only provide a competitive edge but also meet societal and environmental responsibilities—the 'planet, people, purpose, profit' paradigm.

Allow me to explain this with an example from my tenure as CEO of Ohm Mobility, an electric mobility management and solutions provider. Our challenge was to develop a new business model for electric buses (eBuses) and electric commercial vehicles (eCVs). The key issue in the commercial mobility market is the total cost of ownership (TCO). With eBuses costing three to five times more than conventional buses, we needed a model that made financial sense for fleet operators.

Innovative business models like pay-per-mile or decoupling the battery from the vehicle can make eBuses and eCVs more competitive with diesel-powered counterparts. At Ohm Mobility, we implemented an OPEX-based model over a ten-twelve year period, bundling eBuses with connected vehicle packages and charging infrastructure. We even added renewables and battery second life into the mix to ensure full carbon neutrality. For instance, when we deployed 300 eBuses in Bengaluru, they consumed roughly 13 GWH of power annually. We decided to build a 15 GWH solar farm in the state to power our fleet with green energy. An added advantage of this strategy was that we could source renewable power at about INR .80 to INR 1.00 (around $0.010 to $0.012) per unit cheaper than if we just powered it from the normal grid. This not only aligned with our carbon-neutral goals but also reduced our energy costs, thereby boosting our bottom line.

The concept of TCO is crucial in the fleet world, where operators work on razor-thin margins of 2 per cent to 4 per cent. Declining battery prices and rising compliance costs for diesel engines will likely help eCVs achieve cost parity with diesel vehicles around 2026, including in major markets like India, making eBuses even more attractive in the long term. So, for an eBus sold on a ten-year package, the economics will become much more appealing than it will for a diesel equivalent.

These pay-per-mile contracts for eBuses, known as Gross Cost Contracts (GCCs), are gaining popularity. A form of public–private partnership, these contracts bundle everything from vehicles and drivers to charging infrastructure and maintenance. It has taken off in India with more than thirty cities having already rolled out such tenders.

In the eCV sector, large fleets need electrified depots. Companies can either invest in electrifying the depot themselves or opt for a service model known as decarbonization as a service (DaaS). DaaS, which is offered by companies like Hitachi and Siemens, allows businesses to purchase carbon-free energy as a service rather than investing in energy infrastructure. This enables fleet operators to focus on their core business while a third party manages their batteries, energy infrastructure and related expenses.

Switching from an ICE powered vehicle to an EV or moving from fossil fuels to renewables energy to power your organization requires significant investment and is rather difficult to justify with a high CAPEX upfront cost and the associated risks linked to battery life or residual value. In the context of the shift to net zero, DaaS presents a scenario where businesses purchase carbon-free energy in the form of a service[5] rather than investing in the energy infrastructure. So, as a fleet operator, you can focus on your core business of efficiently running your fleet and let a third party manage your batteries, energy infrastructure, and all related expenses to charge your vehicles. The fleet operator, in other words, is renting an energy service.

DaaS can be further enhanced with outcome-based models, where the provider's compensation is tied to the amount of carbon they can remove from the client's operations. Beyond building the energy infrastructure, providers could offer green energy, manage energy-storage systems that contribute to the grid during peak hours, and even generate additional revenue. This model changes the focus from simply providing a product to delivering a performance-based service that aligns with net-zero goals.

UgoWork is one such company offering an energy-as-a-service model to material-handling companies, while SunMind provides solar farm development as a service for clients on their unused property. These OPEX-based models involve zero upfront CAPEX, offer zero-emission operations, and integrate digital and energy solutions powered by green energy, with zero risk to the user.

In essence, DaaS is akin to outsourcing your digital infrastructure to AWS or Azure for cloud services. For fleet operators, it's like purchasing an ICE vehicle without a fuel station, relying instead on third parties like Shell or BP to fuel the tank.

As we march towards a net-zero future, the need for innovative business models that align with zero strategy becomes more urgent. These models—whether pay-per-mile, DaaS or outcome-based—are not just about adopting new technologies. They represent a shift in how businesses operate, focusing on long-term sustainability, reduced environmental impact and financial viability.

Step 7: Lead from the front, spin the team into a separate function, and agree and approve the budget upfront

In my experience, companies that have been able to implement breakthrough zero-vision strategies have been led from the front by a strong leadership team, in most cases by the chairman/CEO of the organization. Consider, for example, Mary Barra who drove

GM's zero-crashes, zero-emissions, zero-congestion strategy, Thierry Breton who spearheaded Atos's zero-email strategy, and Andy Palmer (COO) who steered Nissan's zero-emission strategy.

My experience also shows that a disruptive zero vision is oftentimes accompanied by organizational pushback, much like Andy Palmer faced when Nissan was trying to develop the EV Leaf. It is therefore imperative that you get senior leadership management to buy into the vision and be invested in its success. Like Andy Palmer mentioned, 'provide air cover to the team so they can remain focused on achieving their goal'. But, like most everything in life, converting vision to reality in a way that yields maximum benefit will require everyone in the organization to be on the same page. It will require leadership to provide direction, alignment and guidance in setting organizational agendas for vision zero. It will require employees to be full participants and feel a sense of ownership in the process of transformation. Because, ultimately, it is only through the cohesion of top-down and bottom-up energies that sustainable change will be possible.

In addition, it is best to hive out a separate organization, a subsidiary, or even a separate cross-functional team to achieve greater organizational agility. As highlighted in Nissan Leaf's case study in Chapter 4, the automaker created a separate zero-emissions business unit and pulled in functions from product planning, finance, engineering, R&D and others into this one business unit with its own P&L. Importantly, it also realized that the business would lose money initially, so it was given a separate budget and the board agreed upfront that it was prepared to lose money since the initiative was not about making money so much as achieving a revolutionary breakthrough.

Step 8: Implementation

'Ideas are easy, implementation is hard.'

—Guy Kawasaki

The same goes for implementing the zero-vision strategy.

It was easy for Atos to develop a zero-email vision but extremely hard to implement it.

In order to become a zero-email company, Atos followed a five-phase approach:

1. Creating awareness: Building awareness within the organization about the importance and benefits of zero vision. I would suggest that an organization should go well beyond this step to creating a cost–benefit analysis and a business case. Needless to say, it is far easier to sell an idea or concept, both internally and externally, if there are factual numbers to back it up.
2. Envisioning the details: In the envisioning phase, Atos proposed a roadmap and detailed all the elements needed to help it succeed. For me, this stage would encompass clearly defining the strategy and vision, conducting an organization's maturity and readiness scan, and building a business case and risk/mitigation assessment plan.
3. Pilot phase: Atos then ran a pilot phase where it launched the programme in a contained environment and then proceeded to analyse the quantifiable key performance indicators.
4. Full-scale implementation: Once Atos was happy with the results of the first three steps, it went in for full-scale implementation. This included an internal and external communication plan with a full change-management support structure.

5. Nurture phase: This phase included performance management, continuous learning, adapting, evaluating and improving based on key experiential lessons.

Step 9: Incentivize the vision

I am a firm believer that we humans are inherently greedy and need an incentive to motivate ourselves. It is therefore important that you create an incentive plan for employees to achieve the zero-vision goal. By doing so, you will encourage the entire organization to be engaged in the implementation process. When Atos was executing its zero-emails vision in 2013, 10 per cent of a top-700 leader's bonus was tied to their vision performance. In 2014, Atos added five Key performance indicators (KPIs) for its leaders and managers to make it a success.[6] This turned out to be very beneficial for Atos in its implementation.

Step 10: And, above all, be patient

At times, implementing a transformational vision can take toil, tears, sweat and loads of patience. It took three years for Atos to eke out some results from its zero-email vision. In the interim, many of the company's staff felt alienated. I remember talking to a few employees who hated the change, especially as they were the ones tasked with implementing zero emails. What frustrated them was that while they were going the zero email route, their clients and other stakeholders were not, resulting in the internal organization not being in harmony with the outside world. Atos did not fully achieve its objectives of zero emails in 2013, but it did lay the foundation for the next generation of collaborative and communication tools that we now use so often. So much of our work today is done through just WhatsApp.

Then there's the case of Copenhagen which, in 2012, became the first city to launch a carbon-neutrality plan for 2025. The city recently announced that it would not be able to hit its target because of the inability of a semi-public utility to secure funding for a carbon-capture plant. Copenhagen now expects to achieve carbon neutral status in 2030. One might argue that it has failed to meet its original target, but it is worth noting that the city has made significant progress, reducing its CO_2 emissions by 80 per cent since 2009.

Embarking on the journey towards vision zero can be arduous. There will be delays and disappointments, frustrations and failures. Yet every step forward represents a major gain. The key is to beaver away with persistence, perseverance and patience.

ANNEXURE 1

CHEAT SHEET—KEY QUESTIONS TO ASK YOURSELF IN YOUR ZERO-VISION JOURNEY

I have been asked on numerous occasions by corporates and executives about how to launch a zero-vision strategy. Therefore, I have included a few questions here—a cheat sheet, as my son would call it—to get you started thinking about how to build your zero-vision strategy.

Setting the vision

1. What business are you in? I tell car companies that they are in the business of personal or freight mobility and not of making cars or trucks. How people and goods move will have an impact on your products and services. Once you understand your industry, it is then easier to build a zero-vision strategy embedded within your products and solutions.
2. Linked to the above, does your company have a clear being and purpose, more than just a vision and mission

statement? Does your vision and mission statement clearly articulate your innovating-to-zero intent?

3. Does your business define your business offerings like your products, services, solutions and platforms? This might sound trivial but a product, for example, a car, is providing a service, for example, a ride-hailing service like of Uber's, with a solution, for example, an integrated vehicle, financing and aftermarket offering bundled together with a platform for a fleet company. In short, a scenario where you are providing product/service/solution and more through a digital tool and in collaboration with other participants within the ecosystem. Why is this important for building your zero-vision strategy? Take my example, for instance. During my stint with the Hinduja Group, I helped develop a platform for one of their companies, Ohm Mobility.[1] The platform supported a pay-per-mile service for electric buses, combining a Zero CAPEX solution (it was a fully OPEX model) for customers with a fully integrated and connected energy solution that included setting up a renewable solar farm to offset the energy consumed by the bus fleet. We estimated that our buses in one of the large Indian cities would need 11 GWH of energy every year and we planned to set up a solar farm for 13 GWH, through one of the group's subsidiaries, to cover any energy losses. In other words, a net-zero bus operations. The plan was not only to have a net-zero fleet but also to have better ROI as the cost of renewable energy was cheaper by INR .80 to INR 1.00 per unit.
4. Can your organization's board, leaders, employees, stakeholders and, most importantly, customers understand and articulate the purpose of your organization? Is zero embedded in that purpose?

5. Do you understand the mega trends that are impacting your business directly and indirectly and what impact they have today and potentially tomorrow?
6. Do you understand the unmet needs of your customers?

Defining the goals, the objectives and monitoring

1. Does your vision and mission statement include your innovating-to-zero goal?
2. Do you set short-term and long-term goals, and do you track progress regularly against these long-term goals without moving the goal post? Most zero-vision goals require patience and planning.
3. Do you have companywide environmental, social, governance (ESG) and diversity, social and inclusion (DSI) goals, and do all these goals reflect together as an integrated whole into your organization's offering as opposed to being standalone? For example, as a car company, you might argue that you already make zero-emission electric trucks, so you don't need to do more. But what if you could also engineer vehicles that were easier for women, the elderly and younger people to drive? This would allow you to address the driver shortages faced by the commercial-vehicle industry, while concurrently promoting diversity among the driver cohort. Additionally, you could contribute towards positive social impact by adding certain health, wellness and wellbeing features for drivers on your vehicles. These would enable greater comfort, convenience, and offer advanced driver assistance features based on individual requirements rather than any perceived collective needs.

4. Are you setting ambitious targets for your teams and for yourself, and are these linked to the United Nations' Sustainable Development Goals? Have you linked these goals to your value chain partners, for example, suppliers and channel partners?
5. Do you have a board member and a CXO who is responsible for your ESG and DSI strategy? Expand the role of these individuals to overseeing innovating-to-zero vision and goals.
6. Do your employees have specific and quantifiable sustainability and environment targets? Further expand them by including zero-vision targets.
7. Does your (zero) vision percolate to all the departments and functions of your organization and from the loftiest CEO to the lowliest intern?
8. Does your organization empower the management team to realize long-term benefits for both company and society?
9. Do you have incentives linked to long-term sustainability goals?

ANNEXURE 2

MEGA TRENDS AND FORESIGHTING

Bill Gates once said: 'We always overestimate the change that will occur in the next two years and underestimate the change that will occur in the next ten. Don't let yourself be lulled into inaction.'

Personally, I am a great believer in this viewpoint, having worked in foresighting for over two decades and having also written new mega trends.

Considering the significant impact of longer-term trends, the foresighting team at MarketsandMarkets has developed a framework with twelve of the most significant mega trends of the future. Chart 10.2 shows the MarketsandMarkets Trends Wheel, which lists the trends and sub-trends broken down by horizon.

Horizon 1 refers to trends we are aware of and understand. These are trends that should be in every company's immediate strategic plans. Horizon 2 refers to trends we are aware of but whose implications we don't fully understand. Your organization should be assessing these trends through medium-term planning and adaptation. Horizon 3 trends refer to emerging trends that we are somewhat aware of but are either not yet achievable or whose outcomes remain highly uncertain. These trends look at the long-term future. They may not yet be widely recognized or understood but have the potential to significantly transform industries, societies and economies. Understanding Horizon 3 trends is crucial for organizations because they provide insights into the strategic challenges and opportunities that will define the future and can lead to proactive strategies for long-term success.

Let's look at the twelve mega trends:

1. Hyper-connected world: Each generation of technology has revolutionized how we connect and interact. 3G brought data, 4G brought video and 5G supports B2B use cases like machine-to-machine communication, providing us with connected stadiums, factories and cars. But 6G? The leap from 5G to 6G promises colossal change, bringing isolated entities like homes, cars and cities together into a unified connected living ecosystem. 6G will likely be 100 times faster than 5G and will allow for immediate communications between consumers, devices and the surrounding environment. For businesses, 6G-enabled technologies will unlock new possibilities and drive digital transformation. 6G will also ignite the metaverse by enabling immersive extended reality (XR) experiences. Combine this with Space Jam—we will launch 20,000 satellites in this decade, compared to about 2,000 in the last decade, providing high-speed broadband and possibly 5G speeds in the future through satellites and precise location-based services. On top of this, we will have higher-speed wireless broadband services, moving from the current Wi-Fi 8 with about 46 Gbps speed to Wi-Fi 10 with speeds of around 200 Gbps and potentially to game-changing Li-Fi in the future. In Li-Fi,[1] solid-state lighting

(SSL) such as LED bulbs are used in the transmission of data and is more secure than Wi-fi and doesn't suffer from congestion and multi-user degradation. The future therefore will be connected everywhere, anywhere, anytime, making it a hyper-connected world that will trigger new disruptive business models. The future, in essence, will echo a constant connection. In such a world, being disconnected might be the only true luxury.

2. Dawn of technology singularity: This trend charts the AI evolution from narrow AI to the dawn of singularity, where intelligent and powerful technologies could radically transform our reality with unpredictable results. With the advent of generative AI, I believe we have now entered the general AI era. Generative AI or strong AI models learn from data and create new content by recognizing patterns and relationships within that data, rather than relying on predefined rules. This enhances creativity and innovation by being able to rapidly generate novel content like images, videos, text, and music. Artificial superintelligence (ASI), where AI reaches human levels of consciousness, intelligence and capabilities, is still decades or more away.

   A key sub-trend of the growth of AI and the hyper-connected world will see us entering what we term an autonomous world. MarketsandMarkets believes that anything that moves in the future could be autonomous. This includes anything with propellers, wheels, legs or arms in industries such as mobility, aerospace and defense, mining, construction and healthcare. Autonomous systems move without human intervention by sensing, perceiving, planning and acting on their own. The leap to full autonomy is happening faster than we might expect. While it took around 200 years to transition from mechanical systems to automation, reaching Level 4 autonomy—where systems can operate independently in specified situations—is expected to take less than twenty-five years. Level 5 autonomy, where machines operate entirely without human input, allowing one to drive from Paris to Frankfurt at Autobahn (no limit) speeds in any driving condition while sleeping in a vehicle without a steering wheel or brakes, is at least a couple of decades away, in my opinion, if not more. By 2035, the autonomous world is expected to be a $10 trillion opportunity with around 900 million autonomous units in operation. Of these, over 75 per cent will be Level 3 and Level 4 systems. While household robots, including vacuums, lawnmowers, companionship and elderly assistance robots, will make up the bulk of units, mobility will be the largest market at $4.1 trillion.

By 2035, we will see the advent of new computing sciences like neuromorphic computing, DNA computing and quantum computing. They will further challenge Moore's law and accelerate the shift to super AI, meaning machines could become more intelligent than humans, thereby achieving technology singularity. Whether or when this will be achieved is uncertain, but what is certain is that the AI revolution is here, and companies must be prepared to adapt and thrive in a new era.

3. Industry 5.0—the symbiotic era: Industrial revolutions have profoundly impacted how we live and work. For example, the first industrial revolution shifted the economy from farming to manufacturing and brought about mega trends like urbanization. The fourth industrial revolution is about applying emerging technologies that

are connected, interactive and intuitive, with the end objective of deriving maximum cost and time efficiency.

The fifth industrial revolution, or Industry 5.0, will focus on sustainability and the wellbeing of society. Building on the concepts of Industry 4.0, this new industrial revolution is described by the European Union as providing 'a vision of industry that aims beyond efficiency and productivity as the sole goals and reinforces the role and the contribution of industry to society'. It will bring about an era of humans working alongside advanced technology and AI-powered robots to enhance workplace processes. It highlights a human-centric approach where the significance of human skills and creativity sits alongside advanced automation technologies. The three key pillars of Industry 5.0—human-centric, resilient and sustainable—will have a profound impact on our society at large, where human-robot coworking will reframe the fundamentals of jobs, skills and global sourcing. It also means that companies will need to become part of the solution for sustainability, rather than part of the problem.

4. The energy transition: The future of energy will be decarbonized, decentralized, digital and democratized, and, one day, possibly even free. Decarbonization refers to the shift from fossil fuels to renewable energy sources. Decentralization in the energy sector refers to the growth of smaller on-site renewable power generation solutions. Digitalization refers to the shift from analog to digital solutions in energy infrastructure, like smart meters and smart grids, to real-time management and processing of billions of data points that automate decision-making and allow the integration of diverse power-generation sources. Democratization refers to the localization of energy and

the harnessing of local, natural energy sources to develop the best energy mix for that country/region, while making energy accessible to all.

We at MarketsandMarkets believe that one day in the twenty-first century, energy generation could be free. This would depend on whether the industry is open to change, since this will then usher in new disruptive business models and opportunities that are unique and very different from what we see in the world today. That could mean future fuels like green hydrogen will be abundant if the solar or wind power needed to generate it is free. In this world, power would not be a commodity but a right—a fundamental amenity available to everyone.

5. Future of mobility: The future of travel won't just be faster, it will also be smarter. Imagine a world free from transport woes, where multimodal, integrated systems offer real-time dynamic guidance, culminating in almost instantaneous journeys. The future of mobility will be multimodal, integrated and door-to-door, combining multiple energy-efficient transport modes with mobility-as-a-service (MaaS) platform offerings. Mobility will be an integral part of a zero-vision world, where the three evils of transport—congestion, pollution and accidents—are all eliminated. We will have the fourth and fifth dimensions of travel introduced with sub-surface and super-surface travel, and where hypersonic speeds will be a reality (imagine London to New York in two hours). This scenario will lead to a state of mobility that takes us closer to transcending time and providing instantaneous mobility.
6. Future society and urbanization: A future heterogeneous society will be more diverse in terms of age, sex, culture and wealth, and will require more personalized and

customized services from businesses. While the global population is aging, some nations in Asia and Africa have young, fast-growing populations. We will likely see large-scale migration in the next few decades that will reshape global demographics. This will be a result of climate change as well as declining populations (and demand for labour) in certain parts of the world. For example, by 2050, the populations of sixty-four countries, chiefly in the developed world, will shrink by at least 1 per cent. In contrast, African countries will see their populations double to 2 billion. We will also see more single-person households in the developed world as well as the arrival of megacities, with populations exceeding 10 million. By 2050, over 70 per cent of the world will live in urban centres, up from 55 per cent today. The fastest growth will take place in the developing world, with India adding 416 million urban dwellers and China adding 255 million by 2050. This will drive innovation to support and sustain ever-growing urban environments.

7. Economic powerhouses of the future—baby-boom economies: With growing populations and a youth demographic dividend, many emerging economies will outpace advanced economies in growth. In fact, by 2040, today's developing economies will account for more than 65 per cent of global output. We believe that countries with a 100 million+ population have the potential to be trillion-dollar economies by 2040. Therefore, future growth will be driven by what we term 'baby-boom economies'. In this changing economic tapestry, populous nations like China, India, Indonesia, Brazil, Mexico, Saudi Arabia, Pakistan and Nigeria could emerge as the ultimate economic powerhouses by 2050.

Changing economic dynamics also pose challenges for businesses. As we draw this vision to a close, the grand question is: With global population growth potentially plateauing and the climate crisis deepening, could we see the end of growth as we know it? The answer may lie with the emerging middle class of developing countries. Their aspirations, dreams and economic thrust could carve out a new Middle Earth—a world where their ambitions drive global GDP growth, shaping a future that's as unpredictable as it is exhilarating. Alternatively, in a world experiencing polycrisis, could we move 'beyond growth', that is, a vision where we stop viewing growth as an end in itself and instead see it as a tool for achieving societal goals such as environmental sustainability, reducing inequality, enhancing well-being and improving resilience?

8. Personalization of healthcare: If you ask me what *the* mega trend of the future will be, I would say the personalization of healthcare. Healthcare spending is reaching 20 per cent of GDP in countries like the US and entering its teens in Western Europe—levels that are unsustainable and, in fact, higher than defense spending in many countries. At the same time, there is a marked difference globally, with countries such as India and Turkey spending around 3 per cent of GDP on healthcare. This suggests we will see major shifts in the industry, with value-based care, efficiency improvements in healthcare systems, alternative sites of care (beyond or zero hospitals), and a shift towards wellness and well-being.

The key focus of future healthcare provision will be on personalization. As more data becomes available from wearable and digital devices, healthcare providers will be able to utilize AI and machine learning to personalize care for each patient. The 'quantified patient' will become the centre of treatment pathways, influencing policy and regulatory bodies and mandating collaboration between technology, device and pharma companies. The future of healthcare will also be more about overall wellness and preventing disease rather than treating it. We will also see huge growth in personalized medicine and biologics, hopefully finding cures for diseases like cancer and obesity, as we have recently seen with the success of the weight-loss drug Wegovy, and for diabetes, where the biologic drug Lantus, for example, raises insulin levels in the body to keep blood sugar levels under control.

9. Marketplace everywhere: e-commerce has been increasingly expanding beyond traditional online marketplaces such as Amazon and eBay. A diverse ecosystem of marketplaces is emerging and growing rapidly. For example, social media and messaging platforms like WeChat, Snapchat and TikTok, have also become e-commerce platforms, taking advantage of the huge value created by selling online. But online marketplaces are only just beginning to evolve. We will see new models and monetization strategies, as well as greater personalization to boost the overall customer experience. For example, Temu and Shein are turning online shopping into a gamified experience. Along with games that encourage users to spend more time on the app, they use personalized engagement strategies to hook users, fuelling remarkable growth and outperforming traditional e-commerce giants.

We will also see huge growth in the B2B marketplace. According to the US Department of Commerce,[2] the global e-commerce B2B market is estimated to account for about 30 per cent of all sales in 2024 and is expected to grow from around $24 trillion in 2023 to an estimated $36 trillion in 2026, with heavy industries such as advanced manufacturing, energy, healthcare and professional business services driving the majority of this B2B sales value. The growth in B2B is expected not from the likes of Amazon, eBay and Alibaba but from traditional wholesalers and distributors setting up their own marketplaces and corporates setting up their e-stores..

The definition of the future industrial marketplace will evolve to embrace several services, including cognitive product configurators, customer-relationship–management solutions, e-store and e-commerce, new business-model offerings like subscription services, digital twin and augmented reality (AR)/cinematic reality (CR) capability, marketing and contract account management online, and digital product passports.

The uncertainty here is whether these B2B and B2C platforms could ultimately decimate local retail economies.

10. Sustainability, diversity and inclusion: It is increasingly apparent that a balance needs to be struck between economic growth, environmental care and social well-being. Climate change and loss of biodiversity threaten to unleash widespread disruption among businesses and society, as extreme weather events intensify and natural ecosystems are devastated. There is an increasing collective recognition that social, environmental, political and economic crises are interconnected, and addressing them requires transformational policies and concrete actions that target their root causes rather than just their symptoms.

To live within planetary boundaries, we need new economic models, such as a circular economy or a regenerative economy, that preserve the earth's systems so that humanity can continue to develop and thrive for generations to come. We will witness the widespread adoption of the 4Rs—refurbish, reuse, repair, and recycle.

As a result of these impacts, and reinforced by increasingly eco-conscious consumers, environmental, social and corporate governance (ESG), together with diversity and inclusion, will become progressively more important for organizations. Ignoring ESG will impact the prospects for the long-term survival of businesses. Diversity in the workforce has been shown to improve business outcomes, innovation and agility. Hiring diverse teams and designing for inclusion can improve the impact of products and services.

11. Human augmentation: Technologies that augment human capabilities will enable us to be smarter, stronger and more resilient. For example, we may wear exosuits that increase physical strength or universal language translator earbuds that allow us to communicate in any language. However, the most dramatic developments will come from biological augmentation. Insight into our genomes and advances in IVF technology could allow us to select the most intelligent embryos, while gene-editing technology could give us the ability to eliminate all heritable diseases.

    We expect to see new legal and ethical frameworks that will guide future developments. These developments will impact many industries, none more so than security and defense. Future wars will not be won by those with the most advanced technologies, but by those who most effectively combine the unique proficiencies of man and machine, for example, through brain–machine interfaces. If ethical considerations are not managed at a global scale, we could see a new arms race.

12. Innovating to zero: At MarketsandMarkets, we see every disruption as a gateway to game-changing business opportunities. However, the impact of these disruptions is highly context-specific. Our Foresight team works closely with clients to help them navigate these shifts, understand how change will affect their industries and markets, and position themselves to capitalize on these developments for long-term growth.

Strategic foresight enables businesses to think more creatively and strategically about the future by exploring trends and issues shaping their sectors and society as a whole. Rather than merely extending past data into the future, foresight challenges existing beliefs, values and behaviours to avoid the limitations of a 'business as usual' mindset. It encourages companies to envision new possibilities, fostering innovative strategies like innovating to zero that break away from conventional thinking.

A key benefit of foresight is its ability to anticipate emerging trends and opportunities in industries, giving companies a competitive edge. By gaining a deeper understanding of the complex and uncertain environments they operate in, businesses can identify emerging opportunities, mitigate potential risks, and create informed, robust strategies. This proactive approach has been shown to drive significant results—a scientific study found that 'future-prepared firms outperformed the average with 33 per cent higher profitability and 200 per cent higher growth'.[3]

At MarketsandMarkets, the company uses a variety of methodologies to translate disruptive trends into actionable opportunities for growth. Tools include horizon scanning,

CHART A.1: MACRO TO MICRO PROCESS - MEGA TRENDS TO ENABLERS TO SUB-TRENDS

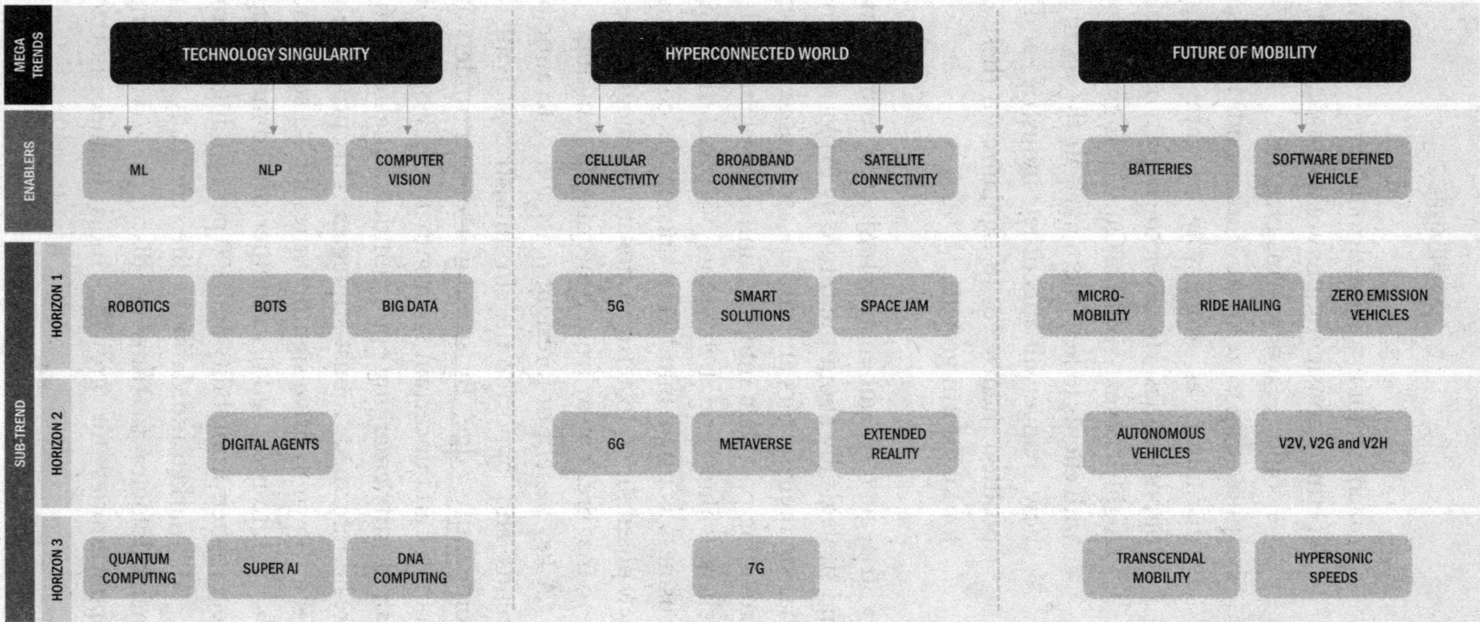

Source : Markets and Markets

visioning and scenario planning. Among these, the approach we most frequently rely on is what we call macro-to-micro. This participatory process helps organizations develop a pipeline of growth opportunities by moving from broad mega trends to sub-trends and finally to highly specific opportunities. Whether it's harnessing hydrogen for local power generation in mining operations or implementing a sensorized smart valve, this method enables businesses to pinpoint opportunities with precision. Chart A.1 shows how we break mega trends to enablers and sub-trends using the example of the mega trends—technology singularity, hyper connected world and future of mobility.

In a world where change is constant, the foresight framework empowers organizations to stay ahead of the curve, transforming challenges into growth engines and positioning themselves for sustained success in an unpredictable future.

ACKNOWLEDGEMENTS

They say you should never make promises you can't keep—especially to yourself. After finishing my first book in 2012, I swore I would never go down that long, bruising path again. Despite my publisher's persistent (and tempting) pleas for a second edition, I held firm, clutching my battle scars from that first round. Writing, after all, can be a test of endurance, and I didn't think I had another round in me.

But fast forward to 2025, and here we are—my second book, *Innovating to Zero*, is now in your hands. I guess time really does heal all wounds. Either that, or I've finally forgotten how painful the first round was. And truth be told, I didn't embark on this literary adventure alone. I had an all-star team around me, and they deserve more credit than I could ever give them in just a few paragraphs.

First and foremost, I owe a huge debt of gratitude to Sandeep Sugla, the mastermind and CEO of MarketsandMarkets, for backing this book from the very beginning. Sandeep is one of those rare breeds of perfectionist visionaries who manages to build global thought leadership in B2B industries, all while making it look effortless. He's an entrepreneurial powerhouse, a market-intelligence guru, and someone who knows how to balance the big picture with an eye for detail. His unwavering support for this book was immediate and generous—he didn't even blink before offering to help. Sandeep, thanks for being the kind of leader who pushes others to be their best.

Now, to the wonderful group of individuals who contributed to making this book a reality: Sidharth Shah, thank you for your invaluable insights on the healthcare section—your expertise made all the difference. Rohit Raghava and Lynne Goulding, you two are foresighting wizards, and your work on the mega trends section was absolutely pivotal. Robert Outram, Lakshmi Narayanan and Neeraj Verma, I couldn't have tackled the chemicals section without your brilliance. To my namesake, Sarvant Singh, your input on the AI section was insightful and, I dare say, mind-blowing. Katyayan Gupta, thanks for navigating the tech section with me—it was no small feat. To Andy Palmer, Shree Das and Tony Stevens: your contributions to the Nissan, Britannia and Tottenham Hotspur case studies added layers of depth that I truly appreciate.

Of course, I have to acknowledge the MVP of my life—my wife, Julia Saini. Julia, I do not know how you've put up with my late-night writing sessions and endless self-doubt. You have always encouraged and believed in me even when I wasn't sure I believed in myself. Thank you for your unshakable support, love and patience.

To my teenagers, Damien and Leyla—thank you for reminding me what's really important and inspiring me to create something lasting. One day, I hope you'll surpass me and write your own bestsellers.

And lastly, I couldn't have made it through this journey without the pillars in my life—my parents. To my Dad, Col. Harinder

Singh, your unwavering leadership and boundless generosity have always been a guiding light for me. Thank you for being the incredible role model you are. Mom, though you're no longer here, your relentless drive (and those infamous 5 a.m. wake-up calls) pushed me further than I ever thought possible. And for that, I'm forever grateful.

NOTES

Scan this QR code to access the notes.

ABOUT THE AUTHOR

Sarwant Singh is a futurist and industry thought-leader with over thirty-one years of work experience in forward-thinking strategic consulting and advisory services.

Sarwant has worked with boards and CXOs of large corporates, as well as the PMO in the UK, to use mega trends to shape corporate growth and future government policies. He has held senior positions in his career, including that of the CEO of a Hinduja-group company, and sits on multiple boards, among them a mobility-focused start-up fund.

Sarwant is the author of *New Mega Trends*, a bestseller in thirty countries, and he has been a regular contributor to several leading publications, including *Forbes*. He is a regular speaker at events and has spoken at COP26 and the World Economic Forum.